THE DANCE
IN CLASSICAL MUSIC

THE
DANCE
IN
CLASSICAL
MUSIC

by PAUL NETTL

PHILOSOPHICAL LIBRARY
New York

Library of Congress Catalog Card Number: 62-18545

Manufactured in the United States of America

CONTENTS

PREFACE   vii

HANDEL AND GLUCK   3

MARIE SALLÉ   7

ARIODANTE   15

ALCINA   17

GLUCK IN LONDON   21

HILVERDING AND ANGIOLINI   25

DON JUAN   31

OTHER DANCE DRAMAS BY GLUCK   35

NOVERRE   39

SONNENFELS   41

THEATRICAL FESTIVALS   45

DANCE IN THE REFORM OPERAS   51

GLUCK'S SWAN SONG   57

MOZART   62

FRENCH BALLET   65

ITALIAN BALLET   77

SOCIAL DANCE: THE MINUET   86

THE CONTREDANCE AND GERMAN DANCE   92

DANCE HALLS   108

THE DANCES OF MOZART   120

HAYDN   137

BEETHOVEN   143

INDEX   163

PREFACE

This book is part of a course, given at Indiana University, entitled "History of Dance Music." In some respects it is a supplement to my book *The Story of Dance Music,* published by Philosophical Library, New York (1947). The present book contains studies on the relationship between music and dance in the works of Handel, Gluck, Haydn, Mozart and Beethoven. I wish to express my appreciation to Anne Lingg, Paul Breed and Bruno Nettl for their help in translating and editing.

PAUL NETTL

THE DANCE
IN CLASSICAL MUSIC

HANDEL AND GLUCK

Handel and Gluck are comparable in a number of ways, in spite of the fact that their lives coincided only partially. They were at least acquainted, if not actually friends, and both were reared in the lap of opera. Gluck, the younger by almost a generation, belonged to a new, pre-revolutionary period, while Handel integrated the achievements of Neapolitan opera, bringing them to a climax and, in a sense, to their conclusion.

In regard to dance, Gluck, essentially a dramatic composer, concentrated on stage ballet, while Handel became a master of dance in many forms not only of ballet, but also of the stylized dances accompanying keyboard and orchestral music. Handel's ballet works were usually composed for specific occasions. A realist, he inserted dances into his operas as demanded by his audiences. In contrast to Gluck, he had no literary advisor and did not concern himself with the problems of expression. Thus his dance music tends to have an improvisatory character. In his Hamburg period he inserted dances in his operas.

The German opera at Hamburg, begun in 1677, wished to offer its patrons public entertainment similar to that of Venice, entertainment which even a semi-educated spectator would enjoy. While contemporary Italian opera concentrated almost exclusively on the cultivation of a beautiful singing voice, the German opera lover preferred the French practice of uniting the various stage arts: poetry, singing, dance, instrumental music, as well as stage design and architecture. Like the Frenchman, he was a rationalist; he could and would not subscribe to the unnatural heroic cult of Roman emperors and Greek gods whose bombastic personalities were all too often expressed incongruously by the graceful rhythm of gavotte and minuet.

According to Johann Mattheson's *Grundlage einer Ehrenpforte* (1740), Handel knew little of melody when he came to Hamburg in the summer of 1703. He had absorbed a scholarly contrapuntal style from his teacher in Halle, F. W. Zachow, but he was willing to learn from the hints of his older colleague Mattheson, as was already evident from his first opera *Almira* (1705). The libretto, fabricated after an older Italian model by a wretched writer, Christian Friedrich Feustking, exemplifies the low quality of Hamburg's literature of the time.

But ballet is not lacking for, immediately after the Rejouissance *Viva Almira* (the opera is a pasticcio), the Spanish gentlemen and ladies dance a chaconne and a sarabande. Musically, both dances are remarkable, especially their trios for two oboes and bassoon. The chaconne is rather extensive and, like the sarabande, uses the *da capo* form. It is worth noting that the sarabande contains a motif which Handel used again in his opera *Rinaldo,* in the famous *"Lascia ch'io pianga"* in the oratorio *Triumph of Time and Truth* (1737), and also in a keyboard suite.

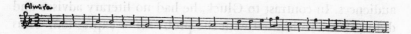

In *Almira,* of course, we find simple, decorative dances which do not reflect any movement of the spirit. The sarabande, however, is a deeply inspired piece. Indeed, both chaconne and sarabande, forms of Spanish origin, express the grandeur of sixteenth century Spain; philologists give the West Indies as their place of origin. This assumption is supported by an etymological explanation of the word Chaconne as originating with the Guacones-dances of Peru. The Jesuit José da Costa, who lived in Peru between 1571 and 1587, describes these as "devil's dances" in his *Historia natural y moral de las Indias* (1590). As late as 1717 Gottfried Taubert, in the *Rechtschaffene*

Tanzmeister (p. 87) mentions the Guacones, according to a treatise, *Historia Morali,* by Homberg (which I have not examined) . A larger ballet in *Almira* is found at the end of Act I, in Scene 11; here the ladies of the court and the state's great personages assemble for word games while pages and lackeys wait on them. Card and dice games are played, but soon the chairs and tables are removed and the dance begins. It is noteworthy that of all the dances included (Courante, Bourree, Minuet, Rigaudon, and Rondo) only the Minuet and Rondo are actually danced, which leads us to believe that the rest were played simply for the entertainment of the audience.

The third act begins, according to the French pattern, with an Entrée in which Fernando, the crown pretender, appears in a horse-drawn carriage accompanied by a large retinue and a choir of oboes. In Scene 2, carried by 12 Moors, appears Osman in a Moorish costume, representing Africa. The African nobles enter, accompanied by a chorus of trumpets and drums, dancing a Rigaudon. It has been repeatedly demonstrated that musical folklore in the Baroque was used without any sense of realism (see the dissertation of my student, Miriam Whaples, *Exoticism in Dramatic Music, 1600-1800*). Handel also does not go beyond setting the Rigaudon in a minor key, giving it a touch of the bizarre.

A dance of the Asians contrasts with the African. Consalvo, in oriental costume, is drawn on to the stage by lions (Scene 3) . Again we hear the "Lascia ch'io pianga" motif, again danced as a sarabande. The next scene features Tabarco, a comic figure on horseback representing foolishness, and ends in a ballet as well, a Gigue with bizarre eighth-note figures in G minor danced by charlatans and harlequins.

The score of Handel's second Hamburg opera, "Nero" (1705) , is lost and only the libretto remains. The text contains 75 arias and, accordingly, the score must have been of considerable volume and no doubt contained a series of ballets. This may also have been true of two other lost operas, "Florindo" and "Daphne." The Hamburg impresario Sauerbrey, who performed "Daphne" in 1708, inserted a gay entr'act entitled "Die lustige Hochzeit und dabey angestellte Bauren-Masquerade," an imitation of the "Carnaval of Venice," presumably in Campra's setting. But we can imagine that the ballet succumbed all too easily to the low level of Hamburg taste.

Handel's next opera was "Rodrigo," performed in Florence in 1707. It is incompletely preserved, for several scenes from the beginning and the end of the score were lost, and the beginning of Act III is lacking. No doubt the overture was immediately followed by a ballet, for after the slow final portion of the overture the score contains a Gigue, a Sarabande, a dance called "Matelot," a Minuet, a Bourrée, an unlabeled Gavotte-like dance, a second Minuet, and a Passacaglia of large proportions. All of these dances, like the overture, are scored in B-flat major, which leads us to believe that nothing intervened between them. The Gavotte-like Matelot is unusual, with its anacrusis of an eighth and a quarter note, its dactyllic rhythms, and its similarity to the Hornpipe. It originated as a Dutch sailors' dance, performed in wooden shoes with the dancers' arms folded behind their backs. Handel's next few operas make little use of ballet, even the famous "Rinaldo" of 1711 has none, at least according to Chrysander's edition of the score.

MARIE SALLÉ

At the end of 1716 and the beginning of 1717, Handel returned to London after a trip to Germany. His interest in opera seemed over, and only at long intervals were "Rinaldo" and "Amadigi" performed. But there are printed announcements which beckon with promises of "several entertainments of dancing," and in them we first encounter the name of Marie Sallé (1707-1756). In the "Daily Courant" of June 5, 1717, we read:

"For the benefit of the boxkeepers, At the King's Theatre —this present Wednesday . . . will perform . . . Rinaldo. With entertainment by Dancing by Mons. Sallé, and Mademoiselle Sallé, his sister, the two children who never performed on this stage before."

This was Handel's first contact with Marie Sallé, who was then nine or ten years old. She and her brother (her senior by two years) had come from France with their uncle, Francisque Moylin, and made their first appearance at the Haymarket Theater on Dec. 8, 1716, in the opera "Cléarte," which had already been performed on April 18. Marie Sallé came from the Théâtre de la Foire (a fair's theater) in Paris, where she had developed her talents of mime and made herself the first "danseuse-mime." To be sure, in the stiff atmosphere of the Paris opera there would have been little opportunity for her talents to unfold. But this finally did happen on the stage of her true discoverer in London, the stage director John Rich. She had also been taught by one of the most famous danseuses of her time, Françoise Prévost, who had ennobled and sublimated her still immature expression. As the daughter of an acrobat she had first participated in questionable performances, and a year after her first London appearance she made her formal debut in the comic opera "La Princesse Carisme." Another personality in London was essential to her development: John Weaver (1673-1760), known as the father of English pantomime. The son of a dancing master of the same name, Weaver was among the first character dancers and a successor to the dancers Luke Channel and Josias Priest, Purcell's choreographer. His favorite ballerina was Hester Santlow (Mrs. Barton Booth). An outstanding clown, he was the principal dancer in the Drury Lane or the Lincoln's Inn Fields Theater from 1700 to 1736.

But Weaver's greatest significance is in the field of the Grand Pantomime-Ballet, in which he was among the first to create a "ballet d'action" and thus was a predecessor to Hilverding, Angiolini, and Noverre. Already on March 2, 1717, he presented "a new dramatic entertainment of dancing, after the manner of the ancient pantomimes, called The Loves of Mars and Venus," with Dupré Sr. as Mars and Mrs. Santlow as Venus, this being perhaps the first original English ballet. In the "Apology" in the libretto, Colley Cibber comments as follows:

"The fable of Mars and Venus was formed into a connected presentation of dances in character wherein the passions were so happily expressed and the whole story was so intelligibly told, by a mute narration of gesture only, that even thinking spectators allowed it both a pleasing and rational entertainment."

Weaver's idea of a rediscovery of ancient pantomime was not well received by the English public, and thus his next pantomime, "The Shipwreck or Perseus and Andromeda," was a combination of his ideas with those of the Commedia dell'arte. In the announcement of his piece he does not refer, as he did for Mars and Venus, to a classical model, but designates his production as "A New Dramatic Entertainment of dancing in

8

grotesque characters." If he was to be successful, he had to keep pace with his rival, John Rich of Lincoln's Inn Fields, who himself had assimilated Weaver's idea of combining dance and pantomime but had, in contrast to Weaver, introduced song and spoken dialogue. Weaver was among the first, not only in England, who thought about the nature of dance. His "Anatomical and mechanical lectures upon dancing" (London, 1721) are the first attempt to base the dance and dance instruction on a knowledge of anatomy. We may assume that Sallé was greatly stimulated by Weaver, who, furthermore, had translated Feuillet's *Choreographie* (1706) into English (1715).

Yet it was John Rich who, in 1725, engaged Marie and her brother along with a group of other Frenchmen who were active in the Théâtre de la foire. At that time already she was famous, indeed, she was considered the equal of Camargo, and Noverre actually preferred her to that most famous dancer of the 18th century. In his *Lettres sur les arts imitateurs* (Paris edition, 1807) he writes: "We have not forgotten the sincere expressiveness of Mlle. Sallé; her charm is still timely, and the affectation of today's dancers of her category has not eclipsed the graceful, gay, but always decent gestures of this affective artist." Noverre further asserts:

"Mlle. Sallé, an extremely attractive and expressive dancer, was the audience's darling. I cannot give the exact year of her appearance, nor the date of her retirement. In 1745, when I began to attend opera, she had stopped performing, but I frequently saw her at her home. Although she left the theater, she continued practicing daily. I was enchanted by her dancing, which was not brilliant, did not stress difficult maneuvers for their own sake in today's fashion, but substituted simple and moving affections for superficial glitter. Its effect was one of gentility, expressiveness, and spirit. Her erotic dance (danse voluptueuse) unfolded with gracefulness and ease, it touched the heart without using leaps or caprioles."

Noverre also tells us that no less a personage than David

Garrick was among her admirers. And Voltaire compares her with Camargo in the following verse:

Ah! Camargo que vous êtes brillante
Mais que Sallé grands dieux est ravissante
Que vos pas legers et que les siens sont doux.
Elle est inimitable et vous êtes nouvelle.
Les Nymphes sautent comme elle.
El les Graces dansent comme elle.

According to the personnel reports of the Paris Academie de la Musique for 1730, which are presented in Vincent d'Indy's introduction to Rameau's "Hyppolite et Aricie," Marie Sallé was also active as a singer in the Paris opera. This activity of hers was also important in the development of her expressive dance, for no doubt she must have acquired a distaste for dance technique for its own sake through her relationship to music. Thus Cahusac (*La danse ancienne et moderne*, The Hague, 1754) praises her performance in "Pygmalion" and "Bacchus and Ariadne," in which she for the first time appeared without hooped skirt and piled-up hair, contrasting sharply with Camargo, who danced in a short ballet skirt while Sallé herself wore the classic "tunique." It is further important in the development of expressive dance that she preferred the pas de deux, first with her brother, then with Laval or Malter, and later with David Dumoulin. The pas de deux now became the nucleus of development for the "ballet d'action." After her London appearance in November, 1734, she returned to Paris, where she had much success in the "Ballet des Fleurs" in Rameau's "Les Indes Galantes," and in the Passacaglia of "Acte Turc" which was her creation entirely. Presumably she also created the "Ballet des Fleurs."

Already Romain Rolland considered it possible that Handel became acquainted with French ballet in Paris itself. In his travels, whose exact routes are unknown, he may have visited Paris briefly and seen French operas. Leichtentritt believes

(*Händel,* p. 751) that the master, in "Alcina," approached the style of French ballet opera as composed by Rameau. Certainly he had heard French operas in Hamburg and Hannover, and his impressions are preserved in the ballets of "Almira" and "Rodrigo."

On November 9, 1734, the "Daily Post" announced: At the Theatre Royal in Covent Garden, this present Saturday . . . will be perform'd Pastor Fido. An Opera; With several Additions, Intermix'd with Chorus's. Which will be preceded by a new Dramatic Entertainment (in Musick) call'd Terpsichore . . . Tickets . . . at Half a Guinea each. First Gallery 4 . . . Upper Gallery 25." This announcement refers to the second period of Handel's opera season in 1734-35, a time of important administrative changes. Handel had separated from his partner, the Swiss "Count" Heidegger. That shrewd businessman had foreseen the downfall of the enterprise and had found more lucrative fields. Handel thereupon moved to Covent Garden, whose owner was John Rich. "Il Pastor Fido" of 1712 has already been performed at the Haymarket in the Spring of 1734, with the addition of choruses from Handel's Serenata "Parnasso in Festa," which had been sung at the wedding of the Prince of Orange with Princess Anne on March 13. The poet of this text is unknown, the music was taken largely from "Athalia," which had not yet been performed in London. The addition of choruses in "Il Pastor Fido" facilitates the performance of the dances.

The pastoral piece was preceded by an introduction entitled "Terpsichore," in which Apollo, sung by Carestini, appeared with the Muses, among whom Erato, "President of the Musick," sung by the famous Strada, and Terpsichore, "President of the Dancing," (Preside del Ballo) by Marie Sallé. Choruses and dances were also included.

Chrysander asserts that "Terpsichore" was an independent, though insignificant, work, "introducing Apollo, who enters in order to inspect the new Academy (Nuovo Museo) but spends his time dancing with Terpsichore and in song declaring his love for her. This type of prologue was chosen because Rich had a very popular dancer, Mll. Sallé, available and she performed her well-known Charactères de l'amour to Handel's music." At the end of "Il Pastor Fido's" first act a chorus of hunters appears, and there follow a march and a "Ballo di Cacciatori." The ballet in the first act, accordingly, has three parts, a march, an "Air pour les chasseurs," and a dance-like piece without title, characterized by swirling figures for the oboes and violins. The "Air pour les chasseurs" is a typical "chasse" with the following melody accompanied by two horns.

At the end of Act II we find a "Ballo di Pastori e Pastorelle" preceded by a "Coro di Pastori." In the score we first find an unnamed movement in cut time.

Then comes a Musette with a drone bass and transverse flute, followed by two Minuets, the first set in three parts, the second in four. Finally, at the end of the opera, there is a "Ballo generale" preceded by a chorus "Replicato al ballo al canto." Handel composed three dances for this ballet, the first and third undesignated, the second a Gavotte with the following tune.

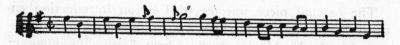

It strikes the listener that the dances in "Il Pastor Fido" are only occasionally French in character. They hardly differ from those of "Almira" and "Rodrigo," tending to be folk-like, especially those in Act I. In "Il Pastor Fido" itself we find only group dances, while the Prologue "Terpsichore" depended on Sallé's solo work for its effects. While "Il Pastor Fido" constantly underscores the relationship between ballet and opera, "Terpsichore" places no emphasis on a relationship

with the main work. Apollo, Erato, and the other Muses meet, excepting Terpsichore, who makes a solo appearance with her "discepoli." This occurs in a Chaconne of large proportions, a piece in Lully's style, with French trios, which were presumably reserved for Sallé's solos. A magnificent piece, it is taken from the danced chorus "S'accenda pur di festa il cor" from "Parnasso in Festa," to which some repetitions and inserts were added. A short prelude precedes the Chaconne, its internal pauses suggesting gestures of special significance.

The libretto and the piano score tell what the next pieces represent. Erato and Apollo sing a duet, "Col tuo piede brilla amor, co'tuoi giri incanti il cor," and from its characteristic melody is derived a Sarabande for strings, danced by Sallé. It is the first of four pieces intended for "Charactere de l'amour," representing awakening love. The second of these "characteres," premonitions of happiness, is accompanied by a Gigue in G major. Then follows an Air in G minor in which Terpsichore expresses the power of jealousy, its feelings of ambivalence clearly shown by constantly changing rhythms and tempo. Finally she presents the force of the winds in an unnamed movement for two flutes and violins, expressly marked pianissimo, a piece not as naturalistic, however, as Rameau's works of this type.

In "Terpsichore," Handel tried to produce a small "Gesamtkunstwerk." In order to produce grand effects he not only used Sallé and her group but also allowed Apollo and Erato to express their passions and feelings, which the orchestra underscores. A G minor duet of Erato and Apollo expresses the hope of a loving, wounded heart: "Tuoi passi son dardi." Besides flutes and strings, he introduces "les orgues" (doucement) and a theorba, with the bass played pizzicato by the cellos.

Handel's way of using music, and Sallé's of making dance express passions, are reminiscent of the Affektenlehre of the 18th century as presented by Mattheson in his *Vollkommener Kapellmeister* (Hamburg, 1739). Of course the types of affects represented by music have a very general character. For example, while the Gigue in G major represents Terpsichore's premonition of happiness, Mattheson gives four main affects for Gigues (p. 228): rage, pride, simple desire, and the flighty soul. Of these the third seems to fit Handel's dance best. Again, while Handel's Sarabande expresses awakening love, the Hamburg critic (p. 230) associates this form with desire for honor, evidently because the Sarabande is a Spanish dance and, in his opinion, Spaniards suffered from an exaggerated concern for honor.

On Dec. 18, 1734, the pasticcio "Orestes" was performed. Leichtentritt designates it as an emergency product, and it does seem a futile attempt of Handel's to combine excerpts from his older operas with a few new pieces into an artistic unit. Chrysander believes that it was chosen with the possibility it presented for inserting dances in mind. Since this work has not yet been published, a commentary is impossible. It seems to have been a failure, because of which the master, who was suffering from depressions at the time, spurred himself to complete a new manuscript in an unprecedented eleven weeks. The resulting "Ariodante" was produced at Covent Garden on Jan. 8, 1735.

ARIODANTE

According to an announcement in the "London Daily Post" (Nov. 4, 1734), Handel had already in November played parts of the score on the harpsichord for the royal couple at St. James's, and the king was not only satisfied but also subscribed 1000 pounds for the following season. Burney also tells us that the opera's main attraction was the dancing of Sallé, whose art competed with the singing of Carestini's Ariodante, Strada's Ginevra, and the Basso Waltz's King of Scotland. The theme was already familiar in opera. The book had been written by Antonio Salvi for Pratolino and Florence with the title "Ginevra," and had also been performed as "Ariodante" in Venice (1716), with music by Polaroli. In 1733 it was again given there, and Chrysander believes that this performance stimulated Handel's use of the libretto.

The plot comes from Ariosto's "Orlando Furioso." The main idea is related to that of Lohengrin. Ginevra, daughter of a Scottish king, is to marry Ariodante, but Duke Polinesso, a discarded lover, tries to prevent the wedding by persuading Dalinda, who loves him and is a friend of Ginevra's, to meet him at night, disguised as Ginevra. Ariodante is made to witness the presumed falseness of his bride-to-be. The others believe him to have drowned himself in despair, and Ginevra breaks down in a faint. Ariodante's brother, Lurcanio, accuses Ginevra of responsibility for the tragedy, but Polinesso offers himself as the defendant of her innocence in a trial by ordeal. Like Lohengrin, a knight with closed visor appears, also as her defendant. He turns out to be Ariodante himself, all is explained, and the story finishes with a happy-end ballet. As usual, the ballets take place at the ends of acts. It is worth noting that a number of arias and even the overture also are dance-like, from which we may conclude that Handel conceived the work as a kind of ballet-opera. This applies especially to Polinesso's aria "Spero," and to Lurcanio's "Del mio sol vezzosi." But even the symphony, scored for two horns, oboes, bassoons, and strings, is a beautiful Barcarole which possibly was danced. It is followed by a Gavotte-like duet of Ginevra and Ariodante which is repeated by the chorus and merges into a Ballo, all of these pieces using the Gavotte theme. Two Musettes follow, then an Allegro in Rondo form, whereupon the chorus is repeated.

The ballet "Entrée de Mori" in Act II uses rhythms from the introduction to Ginevra's aria "Mi palpita." Here we are dealing with one of the Moorish dances whose popularity had been evident for centuries. (Concerning the musico-ethnological significance of the Moresca, see my essay in "Archiv für Musikwissenschaft" XIV, 3.) In contrast to many Morescas of the 17th century, which are general pantomimes and have nothing to do with Moors specifically, this example is a real Moorish dance whose exotic nature is indicated by the hopping movement and the large intervals, music which presumably was intended to accompany Sallé's grotesque figures. This dance is followed by a Rondo, evidently a Passepied which, like the Moors' dance, has no relevance to the plot. The end of Act III is a grande Réjouissance with a massive chorus, followed by a dance which is simply a repetition of the overture's third part, perhaps indicating that it was danced immediately after the overture. There follow a Rondo and an Andante Allegro which also is taken up by the chorus. Obviously Handel here tried to achieve unity in the use of his materials, thus placing himself on a level with Gluck.

ALCINA

The most important of Handel's ballet operas is "Alcina." People who were privileged to hear the rehearsals were overwhelmed, as we can see in a letter written on April 12, 1735, by Mrs. Pendarves to her mother, Mrs. Mary Granville. Having written that she had attended the first rehearsal at Mr. Handel's house, she continues: "I think it is the best he ever made, but I have thought so of so many, that I will not say positively 'tis the finest, but 'tis so fine I have not words to describe it. Strada has a whole scene of charming recitative—there are a thousand beauties. Whilst Mr. Handel was playing his part, I could not help thinking him a necromancer in the midst of his own enchantments."

The performance took place on April 8 at Covent Garden and, again, Strada and Carestini charmed the audience as Alcina and Ruggiero. To what extent Sallé's dancing enchanted the London public we cannot say, for, according to a report by Prévost ("Le pour et le contre") she was hissed at one of the last performances. Prévost's report from Paris, in O. E. Deutsch's translation, says:

"Mlle. Sallé who had at first been as favourably received by the English as Farinelli (however, in due proportion to her talents), found herself afterwards bitterly attacked both in verse and in prose, without anyone knowing the reasons which might justify this change. . . . The opera Alcina was given, the story of which is taken from Ariosto. Mlle. Sallé had composed a ballet in which she cast herself for the role of Cupid and took upon herself to dance it in male attire. This it is said, suits her very ill and was apparently the cause of her disgrace. Her admirers in France will be less chagrined than herself over an incident which may hasten her return to the Parisian theatre, especially since the poor success of her benefit, which did not bring her even half as much as last year."

Just as Ariodante became a kind of Lohengrin, Ruggiero is a sort of Tannhäuser who has left his betrothed Bradamante and is under the spell of the sorceress Alcina. Bradamante releases him from the sorceress's spell. Disguised as a youth, she causes Alcina's sister Morgana to fall in love with her and in turn incurs the hatred of her lover Oronte. Full of mysterious adventure, battles, and sorcery, this opera provides plenty of opportunity for display of grandeur. The dancers first appear in a Musette after the overture, making the spectator's heart caper with Lombardic rhythms and the graceful Minuet following. In Scene 2, chorus and dancers again appear as the magic mountain bursts with thunder and lightning, revealing Alcina's palace. She herself is caressing Ruggiero, holding a mirror, and adorning herself. The singing and dancing choruses consist of young knights and ladies bedecked with flowers.

The chorus "Questo e il cielo di contenti" is taken from Handel's Organ Concerto in F, whose manuscript is dated March 23, 1735. Then follows the Ballo itself, a suite consisting of a Gavotte, a Sarabande, a Minuet, and another Gavotte designated only by "alla breve." These dances have become so popular, having been recorded many times and served as the basis for ballets—Balanchine's "The Gods go a-begging" (1928) and the Alcina-Suite by Andrée Howard (1934)—that it is hardly necessary to describe them here. The Minuet's grace is incomparable. In contrast to Rameau's typically Rococo figures, Handel here combines the Germans' classic melodic line with Italian cantabile and French charm.

At the end of Act II Alcina sings her famous aria "Ombre pallide." When she despairs of other means of keeping Ruggiero's love than her arts of magic, and when she is about to send the spirit of Acheron against him, her magic fails her because her fear, tenderness, and pity prevent her from en-

18

gendering the sufficiently unyielding rage. The accompanied recitative "Ah! Ruggiero crudel" is followed by an aria of despair after which she throws away the magic wand. Then spirits from dreams appear and prepare to dance.

Now it is interesting to find that the words "questi formano il ballo" (i.e. the spirits) are lacking in the 1736 libretto, indicating that the ballet was dropped, Sallé and her troupe having left London. The appearance of these spirits of dreamland immediately upon Alcina's passionate aria seems somewhat forced. We must assume that Alcina, in an unknown aria calls upon sleep to help her forget her suffering. There is the "Entrée des songes agréables," pleasant dreams, who visit Alcina but are soon dispersed by "songes funestes." She awakens restlessly in an "accompagnato." "What have I seen, oh gods! woe is me. I cannot rest and even sleep will not lessen my suffering." Sallé danced in an "Entrée des songes agréables effrayés" and finally in a struggle between the two groups of spirits, in which she expressed all of the beauty and passion, but also the torments, of a nightmare. Especially enchanting is the "Entrée des songes agréables" for string quintet without double bass. By contrast, the dreams of fright are expressed in rushing unison passages. It is possible that Strada's Alcina, while asleep, was replaced by Sallé who, being a former singer, could have sung a short recitative.

The ballet in the last act is also of interest. A group of bewitched persons are freed through the destruction of Alcina's magic power. The libretto explains that Ruggiero smashes Alcina's magic urn, whereupon the stage set disintegrates. The audience sees a grotto in which the bewitched ones resume their human forms, among them Palladin Astolfo embracing his son. This ballet too was omitted after Sallé's departure. In the score, the bewitched ones—Handel's manuscript contains the names of participants: Strada, Young, Wright, Maria Catharina Negri, Boy, Beard, Samuel Howard, Joseph Corf, Waltz, Leveridge, Stoppelaer—awake with a chorus in G minor, "Dall 'orror di notte" ("From the horror of night's darkness, who restores our light and life, gives us back our liberty?") . Composed in a later period, this chorus would have been considered music in the "humanistic style" because of its flowing harmonies and rhythms. Leveridge sings, "I was a forest animal;" Thompson, "I, a rock;" Stoppelaer, "I, a tree;" Howard, "Here as a brook I flowed." The chorus then develops into a pantomime in which the bewitched ones recover the use of their bodies. The theme of creation and regeneration is, after all, one of the deepest and most prominent in drama and ballet, as in Vigano's "Prometheus" or "Pygmalion," in which Sallé performed (London, 1734), or "Pygmalion e Psyche" by Lani, with music by Grauer. Sallé and her troupe dance an Entrée and a Tamburino, the form of which, from the point of view of gesture, seems extraordinary expressive. Simultaneously we recognize in it the influence of French rhythm, as it is frequently used by Lully and his successors in overtures and airs. This serious part is followed by a Tamburino in which the liberated ones express their joy. Orgiastically the piccolo is led over a pedal point. The pantomime's theme develops into the final chorus, "After bitter suffering our souls now live in peace." Combining this chorus with pantomime was one of Handel's great strokes of genius.

Handel's role in the history of ballet began with the purely formal kind in "Almira" and "Rodrigo." But later, under the influence of Marie Sallé, perhaps also under that of Garrick and Weaver, and possibly also through his personal acquaintance with Rameau's operas, he came to use genuine expressive ballet, approaching the style of Gluck and the ideals of Cahusac and Noverre.

GLUCK IN LONDON

Slightly more than ten years had passed since "Alcina" and Sallé's departure from London when Handel met a colleague 29 years his junior, Christoph Willibald Gluck. Gluck had just come from Milan, having presumably been brought by coach via Turin and Paris by Prince Ferdinand Philipp Lobkowitz (1724-1784), whom he had known in Bohemia and Vienna. In 1734 the prince had become regent of the house of Lobkowitz and had attended the imperial coronation of 1745 in Frankfurt. Together with the Duke of Newcastle he had traveled to London by way of Brussels, Antwerp, Rotterdam, Calais, and Canterbury. The reason for Gluck's journey was an invitation from Lord Charles Sackville Middlesex, then director of the Haymarket Theatre. It was simply a matter of finding a competitor to Handel.

Prince Lobkowitz stayed for two years at the Duke of Newcastle's, who had been the British representative at the Frankfurt coronation. From that time stems the information that Handel had told Mrs. Cibber that "Gluck understands no more about counterpoint than my cook," thereby meaning the Basso Waltz. The occasion of this derogatory remark of Handel's is said to have been the performance of Gluck's opera "La Caduta de Giganti," with text by F. Vanneschi, which was produced at the Haymarket on Jan. 7, 1746. It was the first of Gluck's two London operas, the second being "Artamene," first performed on March 4, 1746. Both were pasticcios from Gluck's earlier operas, especially "Tigrane," "Sofonisbe," and "Ipermestra." We learn that Gluck, on April 23, gave a glass-harmonica concert at the New Theatre, playing on 26 drinking glasses tuned by filling with water, accompanied by orchestra. On March 25 there was a concert containing equal numbers of arias by Handel and Gluck, the latter also conducting his own overture to "Caduta de Giganti" while Handel performed a "great concert," presumably a Concerto Grosso.

The occasion of "Caduta's" performance was the Stuart rebellion which had been defeated by a complete victory of the House of Hanover at the battle of Culloden on April 16, 1746. The rebels had, indeed, already begun their retreat, so that Gluck's opera, alluding as it did to the rebellion in mythical costume, was more than timely. Handel, of course, had undertaken something similar in his "Occasional Oratorio." About Gluck's opera itself we learn from Burney that the composer dedicated it to the Duke of Cumberland, the victor over the Scottish rebels. But this is not the place for describing the opera in detail. Suffice it to say that the divas Theresa Pompeati (known through her relationship to Casanova) and Frazi, the singer Ciacchi, and the castrati Angelo Maria Monticelli and Giuseppe Jozzi were among the performers. As a matter of fact Imer, who is mentioned by Burney, is identical with Pompeati, this being the maiden name of the dancer Pompeati's wife.

The star dancer was Eva Maria Veigl from Vienna, who was to become famous as "La Violetta." She was born on Feb. 29, 1724, the daughter of a middle-class Viennese, Johann Weigl, and died on Oct. 16, 1822. When she was still a child, Hilverding discovered her talent for the stage and persuaded her father to educate her for a stage career. When she appeared, she did so under the name of "Violette," alluding to her father's name which is equivalent to Veilchen (the violet) in Viennese dialect. According to Wurzbach (*Biographisches Lexikon des Kaiserthums Oesterreich*, Vienna, 1884, vol. 50), the family goes back to a man who, in the 14th century, presented Duke Otto the Gay with the first March violet and received the surname Veigl. The German poet Anastasius

Grün used this story in a pastoral poem, "Der Pfaff von Kah-lenberg." Eva Veigl made her debut in 1734 in Hilverding's ballet "Amor und Psyche." She aroused such enthusiasm that she was introduced into the highest levels of society and, in 1744, was called to London, where she appeared at the Drury Lane Theater, then directed by David Garrick.

Having an introduction to the Burlington family, Eva Veigl became the teacher of the family's daughter who later became the Duchess of Devonshire. We should remember that Handel, at the end of 1712, had moved to Lord Burlington's palace on Piccadilly, where the empire's best minds, Pope, Gay, Dr. Arbuthnot, Swift, and others met. In the famous struggle between the supporters of Faustina and Cuzzoni, Lady Burlington took the former under her wing. No doubt Violetta became acquainted with Handel. But more important is her relationship to Garrick, whom she married in 1749. Soon after she had accepted her position with the Burlingtons, her health began to fail, and it turned out that she was unhappily in love with Garrick. Lord Burlington spoke to Garrick in her behalf, assured him of a dowry of 6000 pounds sterling which helped the great actor in coming to a decision. Before his death he made Violetta the heiress of his huge estate, with the condition that she must not remarry. She continued to live in her country house at Hampton and died, almost 100 years old, in Shakespeare's easy chair while a companion was reading "Hamlet" to her. Her estate of 70,000 pounds went to her family in Vienna, except for some large gifts to charity. She is described as one of the most virtuous, but also remarkable, women of her time; she received many offers of love but refused them, even the unusual offer of Lord Huntington, who assured her of 50 guineas monthly as long as she preserved her virtue, but who promised her the tenfold amount if she should change her mind in his favor. Her answer is said to be one of the most unusual letters ever written by a woman. At the site of her birthplace today stands the Austrian Kreditanstalt. Although she remained a Roman Catholic, she is buried in Westminster

Abbey at the side of her husband whose coffin reposes under Shakespeare's monument. According to his will, the seventh volume of Samuel Johnson's Shakespeare edition lies on the coffin. The last member of the Weigl family, Franz Weigl, who died in 1866, was a Vienna tobacconist.

In the performance of Gluck's pasticcio, "Caduta de Giganti," according to Burney, the dancing of Auretti and the charming Violetta were better received than Gluck's arias, which Burney remembered, but which are now known only from an anthology by the publisher Walsh. We know nothing of the dances themselves, but since Violetta had been a student of Hilverding's and a great admirer of Garrick's, we may assume that her presentation, like that of Marie Sallé, was directed towards a style of expressiveness. Hilverding played a role of supreme importance in the history of expressive ballet, and Arteaga, the great historiographer of 18th century opera, has ascertained that pantomimic dance was introduced to Europe by Germans, and that it was only later adopted by the French (Chapter 16 in *Le Revoluzioni del Teatro Musicale Italiano*, 1785).

A Court Ballet at the Court of Louis XIII, 1616 (Foto: Archiv Balcar)

Fanny Elssler in the Cracovienne (Foto: Archiv Balcar)

HILVERDING AND ANGIOLINI

Franz Anton Christoph Hilverding, who was born on Nov. 17, 1710, in Vienna and died there on May 13, 1768, was a member of a well-known artistic family. He is first mentioned as one of the 13 "Ballerini di Corte" under the newly appointed ballet master at Charles VI's court, Alexander Phillebois, and in 1742 he became director of ballet at the Kärntnertortheater, where the German plays were given. He created numerous pantomimes and ballets, for some of which Ignaz Holzbauer wrote the music. When the rebuilt Burgtheater gave Gluck's "Semiramide Riconosciuta" on May 14, 1748 (Maria Theresia's birthday) and Hasse's "Leucippo" on Aug. 28, Hilverding received credit for the choreography. This theater was directed by a "Cavalier-Society" under the Impresa of Lopresti. But it became bankrupt and its direction was taken over by the imperial court together with the Vienna municipal government in 1752, with Hilverding appointed as court ballet master at a salary of 600 Gulden, plus 200 for each ballet performance. To be sure, he too suffered financial disaster. One of his dancers from 1742 on was Giuseppe Salomone from Venice, who went to Portugal in 1756 as "Giusepetto di Vienna" and returned to Venice in 1762. About 1746, two other members of the troupe were a son of Salomone's, Franz, and Franz Anton, a son of Alexandre Phillibois. Anton Pitrot from Dresden, who had given guest performances in Vienna from 1750 on, was appointed in 1756. He was joined by the dancers Bernardi, Pierre Lodi (at the Kärntnertortheater) and Gasparo Angiolini (Burgtheater), and

25

about 1754 by the latter's wife, Mme. Geoffroi-Bodin, who had been secured for the Vienna stage in 1752 at the considerable salary of 5775 Gulden. Casanova in his memoirs says that he met the couple in Vienna in 1754, and again in Orleans in 1776. Bodin's wife had become ugly rather than simply old. "Furthermore, she had become pious in deference to her husband, and gave to God what the devil had left behind."

Besides Hilverding, the following were active as choreographers: Franz Anton Phillibois, Joseph Salomone, Pierre Lodi, Philipp Gumpenhuber, Anton Pitrot, and Angelo Pompeati, who was to become second director of the German ballet. Pompeati was the husband of the famous Theresa Imer who, as already mentioned, had appeared in Gluck's pasticcio, and had entered into a relationship with the composer which had almost cost him his health (see Nettl, *The other Casanova*). Pompeati died an unnatural death, as the "Wiener Diarium" of March 23, 1768, indicates: "Angelus Pompeati, former dancer at the German theater, who during an illness wounded himself fatally . . . 55 years old." At that time he had long been divorced from Theresa, who was later to give grand entertainments in London as Mme. Cornelys and who was also the manager of the famous Bach-Abel concerts.

In 1758 Hilverding took leave-of-absence for several years at the request of the Czarina Elizabeth in order to reorganize the St. Petersburg ballet, taking with him the ballet composer Johann Starzer. In the Russian capital he replaced Antonio Rinaldi as maître de ballet, while Starzer was appointed chef d'orchestre. At the Burgtheater Hilverding was succeeded by Angiolini, at the Kärntnertortheater by Bernardi. Meanwhile Hilverding was extraordinarily successful in St. Petersburg, returning to Vienna in 1764 followed by a Russian pupil, "Timoschka" (Timotey Bublikov) and later also by Starzer. In 1766 Angiolini went to St. Petersburg, making his debut with his "Départ d'Enée ou Didon abandonnée," with music by Galuppi. Hilverding too appeared there again, especially on Feb. 2, 1765, with a ballet, "Les amans protégés par l'Amour," which was given as part of a German comedy.

After the sudden death of Emperor Francis I on Aug. 18, 1765, the Vienna stages were shut down, and the Burgtheater not reopened until Nov. 11, 1766. Hilverding received a concession to the Kärntnertortheater and had much success with his ballet "Triumph of Spring." Meanwhile he not only had financial difficulties, he had also become old and ill, for which reason the notorious Afflisio (formerly Beppo il Cadetto) took over the theater in 1767. Casanova had already encountered the foul play of this Neapolitan. A protegé of the Austrian general Prince Sachsen-Hildburghausen, in whose palace Gluck and Dittersdorf lived for some time, he was made a captain and then Count Durazzo's successor as director of the Burgtheater. Casanova had introduced the Prince to Afflisio and, like many an Italian adventurer of the period, the latter had succeeded in getting a foothold in Viennese literary society. It was he who appointed the ballet-master Jean George Noverre. But Afflisio did not remain long in Vienna. When Casanova met him again in Bologna, he was again director of a theater, but he sank lower and lower, ending his days as a galley slave.

On Jan. 11, 1767, the famous Gaetano Vestris (1729-1808), like Noverre a pupil of Dupré, appeared at the Burgtheater in the pantomime "Medée et Jason" with music by J. J. Rudolph; and on Sept. 9 or 10 of the same year, Noverre's "Apotheose d'Hercule" was given as an insert in Hasse's "Partenope," with Vestris as guest star. Still on Dec. 26, 1767, Hilverding witnessed Noverre's insert in Gluck's "Alceste"— "dans le gout grotesque."

Unfortunately our insight into the character of these choreographers is limited, and we are dependent on occasional remarks by contemporaries. Nevertheless we are told that Hilverding's ballets at the Kärntnertortheater concentrated on light and popular subjects, that he introduced peasants, shepherds, soldiers, gardeners, and craftsmen as characters, among them Austrian and Viennese types, Tyrolean woods-men, scenes from Leopoldstadt. Like Rameau, he often used Dutchmen, Spaniards, and Turks as characters. Let us not forget that Vienna had already seen rural types in ballet—Swabian peasants and girls, figures from the Commedia dell 'arte—as introduced by the Venitians Santo and Domenico Ventura (died in 1694). Ventura, a pupil of a student of Beccaria's and a spiritual descendant of Cesare Negri's found a musical helper in Johann Heinrich Schmelzer, who composed native Laendler called "arie viennesi." In the 18th century people were especially inclined to use persons from distant countries or exotic cultures as characters in drama, and especially in ballet. The "noble savage" fits well into a century which loved the exotic, and the Turk with his harem was especially popular. Egyptian settings were not lacking either, but from various titles it is evident that Hilverding was already concerned with expressive dance, as indicated also, for example, by a remark of his pupil Angiolini in the preface to "Le Festin de Pierre:"

"If the public does not wish to rob itself of the greatest beauty of our art, of expressive dance, then it must become accustomed to being moved to tears. This has not happened so far, with the exception of the pantomimes at our theater presented by my master, the famous Herr Hilverding."

Thus we come to Hilverding's pupil, Gasparo Angiolini (1723-1796), the great innovator in pantomimic ballet, who together with Noverre created tragic ballet. Working first in Florence, he appeared in Venice and Turin as "Angelini di Firenze" from 1748 to 1750. After being a guest performer in Vienna he was appointed there permanently in 1757. His wife, the famous dancer Maria Teresa Fogliazzi, followed him to Vienna, where she too had been a guest artist. There she encountered Casanova, who fell unhappily in love with her and who, at her departure, pilfered a portrait of hers which he was later obliged to return to Venice. Between 1759 and

1764, Mme. Angiolini gave birth to five children, of whom Peter (1764-1850) became known as a choreographer.

From the titles of his earliest ballets, according to diaries by the Counts Khevenhüller and Zinzendorf, it is evident that Angiolini was at first a performer of the simple, popular ballet. Then, however, he met Gluck and Calzabigi, the latter having lived in Vienna since 1761, while Gluck had been associated with the imperial court from 1754. Concerned about a reform of opera for years already, Gluck must have been greatly attracted by Raniero Calzabigi's new ideas on the aesthetics of opera. We cannot discuss the influence of this writer and philosopher (who, with his brother and his special buddy Casanova had once been a lottery undertaker and involved in poison-murder trial) on Gluck's reforms. Like many of his contemporaries, he was entranced by the idea of combining Italian and French opera styles. As a counter-force to the libretti of Metastasio, with their intrigues and refined complexity, he proposed to use simple, unified plots for expressing great humanistic ideas. In this respect he is a disciple of Diderot's, especially of his *Le neveu de Rameau* (German translation by Goethe, 1828), according to which operatic singing must reproduce the passions in their natural means of expression.

Declamation is the model for singing, and dance has an important place in musical drama, says Diderot, but in his opinion they must be completely revised. Calzabigi had similar ideas, he wished to use chorus and ballet to the fullest extent possible. If it is true that Angiolini's preface to his ballet "Le Festin de Pierre" was, although signed by the dancer, actually written or edited by Calzabigi (see Ghino Lazzeri, *La Vita e l'Opera Letteraria di Ranieri Calzabigi,* Citta di Castello, 1907), we must ascribe to him a great deal of the credit for developing pantomimic ballet. It seems that Angiolini, Calzabigi, and Gluck developed the idea of the tragic ballet simultaneously, Calzabigi basing his thoughts not on Diderot, however, but on

29

the writings of Cahusac, who in turn went back to Charles Batteux. In Chapter 2 of the third part of Batteux's book, *Les beaux arts reduit à un même principe* (1746), the latter asserts that every kind of music and dance must have a meaning. It is the task of literature, music, and dance to transmit human dealings and passions, for all art—and he cites Aristotle —must be an imitation of nature.

Cahusac, who published *La dance ancienne et moderne ou traité historique sur la dance* at the Hague in 1754 (a German translation appeared in 1759 in *Sammlung vermischter Schriften zur Beförderung der schönen Wissenschaften und freien Künste*), defines dance as "l'art des gestes," in which definition he had a predecessor in Abbé Jean Baptiste du Bos's (1670-1742) *Réflexions critiques sur la poésie et la peinture*. According to Cahusac, the various body movements are carriers of human passion. He criticizes the fashionable dance style of his time, crying, "We have stages on which one can see majestic steps, beautiful legs, and admirable arms. What a shame that we know nothing of dance as an art!" It is he who foresaw the "dance d'action" as later practiced by Marie Sallé. The modern dancer, he says, must be an artistic personality, not a master of dance in the ordinary sense who knows only the conventional steps, movements, and gestures. A dance is an independent creation uniting poetry, music, and painting. In other words, a predecessor of Wagner and the Gesamtkunstwerk.

DON JUAN

On Oct. 17, 1761, the first Vienna performance of a dramatic ballet took place: "Festin de Pierre" or "Don Juan" by Gluck-Angiolini at the Burgtheater. But the audience took offense. How, people asked themselves, can one present this story of horror and tragedy as a ballet, a form in which we are used to seeing beautiful ballerinas and graceful leaps? Still, the piece did in time become a drawing card and the performance of Nov. 3 was sold out. On that day the Burgtheater was completely destroyed by fire, just as the Kärntnertortheater was to be gutted during a performance of the "Tales of Hoffmann" almost 120 years later. Since then, superstitious Viennese theater patrons have been frightened of gloomy subjects.

The Vienna premiere was followed by performances in Paris, Parma, Turin, Naples, Milan, Pavia, Munich, etc. "Don Juan" had to be recast repeatedly (in Paris the original three scenes were expanded to four). Two English arrangements, one of 1785, the other 1787, are preserved in print in the British Museum; one was scored for harpsichord, violin, and flute by F. H. Barthelemon and published by Longman and Broderick, the other was an arrangement of Gluck's themes by W. Reeve.

It might well be mentioned here that 1787 was to be a real "Don Juan" year, the theme being used for a ballet in London, for an opera by Gazzaniga premiered in Venice on Feb. 5, and for Mozart's masterwork which was first performed in Prague on Oct. 29. The famous Sara Goudar took part in the London performance and found the music "admirable" (*Oeuvres mêlées*, Amsterdam, 1787, II, p. 13).

Don Juan also came to America, appearing in a libretto

published by Matthew Carey in Philadelphia on Dec. 22, 1792, entitled "Don Juan or the Libertine destroyed—A grand pantomimical ballet in two parts, as performed with great applause by the Old American Company at the theatre in Southwalk, first American edition." The libretto was also announced in the "Columbia Sentinel" in Boston on Dec. 12, 1795, a journal in which William T. Blake published a series of librettos. We cannot say for sure whether this libretto could have been a pasticcio from Mozart's opera, which had been performed in London in 1791, or whether we are dealing with a ballet-pantomime by Delphini, with music by W. Reeve. There are also, by the way, various modern versions of Don Juan, one by Eric Alladini and Michel Fokine, which was performed in London's Alhambra Theatre by René Blum's Ballet Russe in 1936. Another version appears in a piano reduction published by Universal-Edition, based on a performance by Heinrich Kröller at the Vienna Staatsoper and the Salzburg Festival, a performance which used the original score by Gluck (published by Haas in *Denkmäler der Tonkunst in Oesterreich,* vol. 60) as well as pieces from "Alceste" and "Armide." Professor Haas has pointed out a degree of thematic unity in the music of this ballet, comparing it to variation technique in Beethoven's "Prometheus." Hans Joachim Moser, however, asserts that Haas goes too far in designating the score as a set of free variations on the theme of the first number:

It would be better, also, to designate No. 7 (Gavotte) as a kind of character-bound Leitmotif.

We are tempted to trace the connections between the principle of variation-suite and ballet, for we would find that ballets were danced already in the Renaissance with the music of variation-suites, as, for example, in a suite by Antonio Brunelli (which I presented in "Zeitschrift für Musikwissenschaft" II, No. 7) or in Monteverdi's "Ballo delle Ingrate." It is obvious that Gluck, the keen musical thinker, wanted to create melodic unity to correspond to Calzabigi's ideal of unity of action. The music is full of images. The overture, which is in one movement like those of Noverre's composers Deller, Rudolph, and Starzer, brings on the romantic atmosphere of Don Juan. In No. 1 he enters a Madrid square at night, in No. 2 he serenades Donna Elvira on the oboe. In No. 3 we see the Komtur, his honor wounded, discovering his niece with the Don. His mood is reflected by the anacrusis of 64th notes with wide intervals.

No. 4 represents the Komtur's accusations and Don Juan's evident nonchalance.—But it is useless to try to describe in words the tone painting in this ballet. But let us mention that it influenced even Mozart, as can be deduced from the Minuet, No. 21, which takes precedence to the famous one in "Don Giovanni."

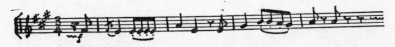

No. 19 too was probably a model for Mozart, in this case the Fandango in "The Marriage of Figaro."

It isn't certain whether the melody is actually by Gluck, or whether it is of Spanish origin and was perhaps generally popular in Vienna, having appeared in a textbook for gymnastics, Gerhard Ulrich Vieth's *Versuch einer Encyklopedie der Leibesübungen* (1794-1818). It is possible that Beethoven, who wrote it down in a notebook of 1810 (see Nottebohm, *Beethoveniana II,* p. 281)—it appears among sketches for the F-minor Quartet—had read it in Vieth's book.

Casanova danced the Fandango in Madrid, described it in glowing terms, saying that he had so far seen it danced only on stage, which may mean that he knew Gluck's "Don Juan." As a matter of fact, this is not the only dance of Spanish origin which Gluck introduced into his ballet. No. 22 has a definite similarity to the Matachin which Pedrell describes in his *Cancionero Musical Popular Espagnol,* a melody which also appears in the *Parodies du nouveau théâtre* (1731, vol. I, No. 48).

"Don Juan's" climax is the third act.

OTHER DANCE DRAMAS BY GLUCK

Gluck composed a number of other ballets besides "Don Juan." According to Khevenhüller's diary, the pantomime "Semiramis," with choreography by Angiolini, was performed on Jan. 31, 1765. Max Arend discovered the scenario in "Hamburger Unterhaltungen" of Jan. 31, 1766. Wotquenne considered the work as of doubtful origin, but already Arteaga considered its authenticity proved. By no means, however, must this ballet be confused with Gluck's opera "Semiramide riconosciuta" (1748), whose librettist was Metastasio. The ballet deals with the legendary queen of Assyria, daughter of Derketo, the goddess of war and passion, the wife of Ninos and after his death regent and builder of Babylon, whose famous hanging gardens she created. According to legend, she killed each of her lovers and when her son Ninias tried to murder her, she became a dove and escaped.

This subject was used in countless operas, and Metastasio's libretto was used by Hasse, Porpora, and Nicolo Jommelli, the latter adding to it a ballet, "Le Feste Persiane" (Stuttgart, 1762). In Gluck's ballet "Semiramis" the queen sees her murdered husband Ninos in a vision, the scene being accompanied by music which was later used as the overture to "Iphigenie in Tauris." In Act II she almost marries her son Ninias (the Jocasta motif) but is prevented by a priest. Finally her son, failing to recognize her, kills her. It is understandable that Gluck furnished this score, which originated about the time of "Alceste" (1769), with the strongest possible expressive devices. Of the 14 numbers there is hardly one which fails to convey the overpowering tragedy of the plot, and Moser is justified in comparing the gloomy grandeur of the music to Beethoven and Cherubini. Harmonic shifts like those in No. 1 (Wotquenne, p. 180), in which the queen's dream is first presented, or in No. 5, give an indication of the intensity with which music and dance are entwined. The music alone would justify a revival of this ballet, but the horror scenes would have to be revised to suit the taste of modern audiences.

The origins of the ballet "Alessandro" are subject to differences of opinion. Several copies with the title "Il Convito d'Alessandro" are extant (Dresden, Berlin, Darmstadt, Brussels). Its eight ballet numbers are hardly enough for an independent work, not to speak of filling an evening's performance. It is praised in the "Wiener Diarium" of 1766, its presumed year of composition. Haas, however, disagrees, believing it was premiered in 1772 or 1773.

In the season of 1771-72 several of Handel's works were performed in Italian in Vienna under the stimulus of Baron Gottfried van Swieten (1733-1803), who had been the Austrian ambassador at the Berlin court and as such had associated with musicians like C. P. E. Bach, Marpurg, and Kirnberger, who introduced him to the works of J. S. Bach and Handel. After his return to Vienna he instituted a sort of Handel-revival in which Mozart also participated, having re-orchestrated several oratorios including the "Alexander-Feast."

When Burney visited Gluck in Vienna in 1772, the composer told the English music historian of his plan to compose a new ode for St. Cecilia's day. Although he thought highly of Dryden's approach, Gluck wished to recast the work into dramatic form so that the singers could enact their passions. The drama was to begin with a feast in honor of Bacchus, with Alexander and Thais present. Timotheus was to appear and sing before them, after Alexander and his beloved have given opposing views of art. Thais disparages the greatness and importance of art, while Alexander believes art's merit to exceed even its reputation. The dialogue is animated by this argument and entertains the spectators until Timotheus appears.

The latter then sings about the Trojan War and moves Alexander to bewail the fact that he, unlike Achilles, has no Homer to sing of his deeds. We know nothing about this cantata beyond Burney's statement, and it would seem that the Alexander ballet, which consists of Introduzione, March, Andantino, Allegretto moderato, Minuet, and Chaconne was to have been inserted at various points. Thus we can imagine the March as martial music somehow reflecting the Trojan War, while the Chaconne was evidently the work's closing number.

A fourth ballet of Gluck's is "L'Orfano della China," again staged by Angiolini. In his diary, Zinzendorf mentions the failure of the ballet "L'orphelin de la Chine" on April 1, 1774. It was based on Voltaire's tragedy "Orphelin," one of the so-called Chinoiseries which were stimulated by the publication of Père du Halde's monumental series, *Description géographique, historique—de l'Empire de la Chine et de la Tartarie Chinoise* (1735). Du Halde published a version of a Chinese play in a translation by Père Brémaire which had also, by the way, been used in Metastasio's "Héroé." The original Chinese play, "Tchao Chi Couell," deals with the saving of the last remnant of the noble family Tchao through its faithful servant, who sacrifices his own child in place of the noble orphan. It also covers the orphan's later life and the family Tchao's rehabilitation through the Chinese emperor. Voltaire's version differs from this one by its secondary use of the orphan, and by its emphasis on the contrast between high and primitive cultures. Tartars and Chinese confront each other. Genghis Khan, who had successfully besieged Peking, had been refused by Princess Idamé, for she was married to Zamti, her family's faithful servant. The Tartar then demanded her as the price of sparing her husband, her child, and the noble orphan, but he is converted by Idamé's spiritual greatness, for she prefers suicide with her husband. Known throughout Europe, this piece was given at London's Drury Lane and plays a part in Garrick's life (see Arthur Murphy, *The Life of David Garrick,* Dublin, 1801, p. 221). The contrast of Tartar and Chinese must have been an attraction for composer and choreographer alike, as No. 4, a march characteristically marked "Barbaro e Maëstoso" clearly shows.

In contrast to the warlike barbarians, the Chinese are represented by a shimmering texture strengthened by Murky-basses in pizzicato. The contrast of male and female (Genghis Khan and Idamé) is shown by melodic antithesis in No. 7. In No. 9 the war-weary Khan and his aggressive general Octar are evidently supposed to appear. But it is difficult to coordinate each piece with Angiolini's choreography. Certainly he, himself a composer, allowed the musicians much more freedom than did Noverre. In this respect the variation-like relationship of Nos. 14 and 15, already encountered in "Don Juan," is worth noting. But "Orphelin," which was given on a bill with "Isola d'Alcina," was no success, and Zinzendorf says of it, "Musique de Cabaret, Pantomime d'un froid à mourir, point de danse." Maria Theresia wrote to Duke Ferdinand on April 12, "Angiolino nous a régalés de deux très mauvaises ballets. On les a sifflés." Angiolini had just returned from Russia and had no easy time competing with Noverre. Indeed, Zinzendorf writes that Noverre, in December of 1773, satirized Angiolini in a ballet (see Reichardt, *Theaterkalender 1775,* p. 43).

The question of priority in the invention of dramatic ballet can perhaps be answered in favor of Noverre by a letter written by Calzabigi to Count Alfieri in 1784: "In 1762, when Medea, the Death of Hercules, and other pantomimes of Noverre's had already been produced in Stuttgart, a work of Angiolini's, Convitato di Pietra, was given in Vienna. Gluck wrote the music and I the French programme, which I introduced with a few notes on the pantomime of the ancients."

A discussion of Gluck's relationship to Noverre is relevant here. In 1747 Gluck was conductor of a traveling opera troupe under Pietro Mingotti in Dresden; Noverre, who lived in Berlin as a solo dancer, participated in the troupe's production of Hasse's "La Spartana generosa." The title role in "Semiramis" was taken by Noverre's pupil Lenzi (who married Antoine Trancard). After Angiolini had gone to Russia in 1766 and Afflisio had engaged Noverre for Vienna, the latter and Gluck worked together intensively. Thus, regarding the rehearsals for "Alceste" in Dec., 1767, Noverre reports that Gluck worked over the statuesquely inflexible chorus and finally called out in despair, "Deliver me, for heaven's sake, give this automaton some life!" Noverre suggested dropping the chorus, but Gluck would not. Finally Noverre is said to have come upon the idea of having the chorus sing back-stage while the action was performed by dancers.

Gluck and Noverre were also on close personal terms, as indicated by a letter of the master's to his friend Franz Kruthoffer, secretary to the Austrian ambassador in Paris, written on Aug. 29, 1776. It concerns the Singspiel "La siège de

Cythère," composed in 1759, which was later produced (but unsuccessful) as "Cythère assiegée" in the Paris Académie Royale. Gluck was not present, having been forced by illness to return to Vienna. Indeed, he had not even been able to complete the score, and one of the Opera's directors, Pierre-Montan Berton, had undertaken to complete the ballet music for the work's final scene. From Favart's one-act vaudeville comedy was fashioned an opera-ballet in three acts, with recitatives and long dance numbers. The first performance on Aug. 1, 1775 was a failure, however, and Gluck swore to compose no more "Ballettarien," and especially no final ballets if they were not integral parts of the plot, even though the French always expected them. "And if people do not accept this, then I shall make no more operas, for I won't have all the papers saying that my ballets are weak, mediocre, etc. The jackasses shall hear no more from me, and my operas will always end with singing."

"Cythère assiegée" was of special concern to Gluck, and when he heard that Noverre was to be in town, he wrote as follows on Aug. 9, 1776: "I hear that Mr. Noverre is to be engaged at the Opera. If this is so, I shall, God willing, be able to produce 'Le siège de Cythère' again, for it will be greatly enhanced by appropriate dances and I have no doubt that it will be a success." But nothing happened. The French would not budge from their opinion that Gluck, in Noverre's words, "would always be mediocre when attempting anything but tragedy." In the new version of "Cythère" he used a slightly shortened version of the first and last movements of the overture to "Paris and Helen." After Daphne's arietta "Habitants de ce doux empire," two Airs de ballet are inserted, the second a sort of trio to the first. After Chloë's aria "Adonis est fait pour charmer" we hear an "air gracieux" taken from "Don Juan," while the Minuet following it is from "Iphigénie en Aulide." Other pieces are taken from the "Alessandro" ballet, from "Semiramis," and the final Passacaglia stems from "Paris and Helen."

SONNENFELS

This is perhaps the place to cite a statement from *Briefe ueber die Wienerische Schaubühne* by Joseph Freiherr von Sonnenfels (1737-1817). The son of the Jewish scholar Lipmann Perlin, ennobled in 1797, he was among the first to spread the ideas of the enlightenment in Austria. His significance is equally great in art and in criminology. The author of numerous literary works, he was also a critic of the Viennese theater and, like Lessing, he was in the vanguard of the battle for good taste in Austria. He was particularly interested in Gluck, and his review of "Alceste" in Johann Adam Hiller's "Wöchentliche Nachrichten" is also found in his *Briefe über die Wienerische Schaubühne* (*Gesammelte Schriften* V, p. 162).

We are indebted to Sonnenfels for an exact description of Noverre's "Les petits riens," which was produced in Vienna in 1786 with music by Franz Asplmayer, and which Mozart also composed in Paris in 1778. "'Les petits riens,'" writes Sonnenfels, "is the neatest piece of its kind ever seen on that stage." But just as Baron Melchior Grimm neglected to mention the composer of the 1778 version, Sonnenfels fails to name Asplmayer. Instead, however, he goes into great detail on Noverre's ballet personnel, and since this interesting contribution has not been published since 1784 it is presented here in complete translation:

"Lenzy has been a great loss to Noverre and to ballet. This excellent danseuse, they say, was a failure in St. Petersburg. The worse for the Petersburg audience! She has the ability of creating enthusiasm for the art of pantomime in an audience completely ignorant of the art's fundamentals. If she was not the object of a conspiracy, then I don't think much of the taste and sensitivity of the St. Petersburg citizens. Lenzy possesses expressiveness to the highest degree; her positions are the noblest in her art, her transitions quick and comely, her gestures full of variety and charm. The lightness of her step and her sureness hide the slight fault in her left foot, which does not point outward sufficiently and is an obstacle during the turns. But who except a jaundiced critic with furrowed brow can occupy his mind with such a slight fault in the face of so many charms?

"Burnonville has also not been replaced. She showed great promise in Medea with her strength of expression. Her most outstanding point was her swiftness, which fits her best, I believe, for lively rather than heroic roles.

"Ricci, a young danseuse who is being trained by Noverre, may well become more than Burnonville. She carries her well shaped body with grace. Her ear is good and is properly obeyed by her well-shaped, light, and well-placed foot. Her excellent entrechat and all other mechanical accomplishments, which she already possesses with some degree of perfection, cause the spectator to wish that she would also enliven her body with the power of drama.

"Besides Ricci we have no female dancers who deserve special mention. But the entire chorus is a selected group equal to none and lends great splendor to our productions. Noverre himself has formed this chorus and directs it in the most charming ensemble dances imaginable.

"Then there are two girls, the bigger of which, Descamps, would be a treasure on any other stage. And indeed, her talent for high ballet and her large stature are not encouraged sufficiently because people are overwhelmed by the charm of her smaller colleague. The latter, only eleven years old, is not only full of promise, she is already a great dancer, uniting all of the talents which Terpsichore commonly bestows only singly on her favorites. In the heroic, in the comic, in gesture and expression, as well as in that which one commonly calls dance proper, which consists of lightness, swiftness, sureness of step, of the height and glitter of the entrechat, of the strength of toe action, even in the facial expressions which describe joy, sadness, discouragement, humor, all passions and combinations thereof, in all these she amazes all spectators and discourages every competitor. One cannot be more richly endowed by nature than she: a good figure, strength in the knees especially evident in leaps and pirouettes—her tendons react like springs, she can stay on tiptoe unbelievably long. Her black eyes speak, showing lively feelings which command her facial expressions and gestures. She holds her arms beautifully and her head posture is the world's most charming.

"People have been concerned that the comic roles, which she has been assigned in various ballets, might hurt her ability to play serious roles. But not in the least is this the case. The latter type are her element, but she can change from the role of a peasant girl to a representation of Psyche or Clytemnestra without the slightest difficulty. She has even descended to the grotesque, and she is an excellent satirist without losing her fundamental nobility and elegance. Foreign readers will consider this description a piece of exaggeration, but I have said nothing which every local spectator would not agree with. This girl, developed by Noverre, is truly her master's pride. (She died before her 18th birthday.)

"Among the male dancers we have lost none of importance during the past year. Trankard is expendable as long as Pik and Simone are present.

"Pik is the most charming youth imaginable, built in nature's most beautiful proportions to the advantage of art: arms, head, thighs, all have the touch of true beauty. I shall not enumerate his talents; he possesses them all, but especially that which the French call 'Moelleux,' and which signifies gentle and flexible bending of arm and sinew whereby sharp and sudden movement is avoided. His beautifully formed face is suited to all but the more violent expressions. It is not strong, not exaggerated enough, to impart slight but important changes in meaning to an audience seated at a distance. Theatrical forms must always, like advertisements, be a bit colossal; and expressed through youth's tenderness they can be brought down to their proper dimensions.

"Simone is good competition for Pik; his entrechat has considerable height and brilliance, his knee bends with strength, and his toe-step is thus best suited to vigorous roles such as those of tyrants.

"The male chorus is a group of skilled dancers, some of whom could honorably hold solo spots on other stages. These are the tools with which Noverre must presently execute his ballets. Note that among his lacks is a mature danseuse able to carry both comic and serious roles, and that this puts a limitation on his planning of the ballets. He must often subordinate the main plot to the episodes since he has good personnel for the latter but not always for the former.

"This year we have been entertained by ballets of all genres: the deification of Hercules, Psyche, Venus, shipwrecks, trivialities, Don Quixote, the benevolent fairy, the vineyard, Flemish festivals, etc. I simply wish to give an indication of the latest subjects, which are not yet known from Noverre's letters."

THEATRICAL FESTIVALS

Gluck did not come upon his ideas of opera reform suddenly, or simply through his acquaintance with Angiolini and
Calzabigi, and thus upon his full use of ballet in opera. We
have seen that already "Caduta di Giganti" contained dance
by Violetta, and several of his pre-reform operas have evidence
in the librettos, if not in the scores, that ballets were performed
at the end, and that they had some relevance to the plot. In
the opera "L'Innocenza giustificata," performed in Vienna on
Dec. 8, 1775, the plot deals with the Vestal Virgins of ancient
Rome, a plot already used by Minato and Draghi in the
Vienna of 1673, and which was to be taken up again by
Spontini in 1807. One of the Virgins, condemned to death
for the loss of her chastity, demands a trial by ordeal. The
opera was recast in 1768 and produced at the Burgtheater as
"La Vestale." Its relationship to the reform operas consists of
the simplicity of its plot and the lack of intrigue and politics.

Unfortunately the dances from both of its parts are lost. But
the libretto indicates that a "Ballo di Nobili Giovanni a Don-
zelle Romane" was included, as well as a ballet of priests and
Phrygian priestesses accompanying a portrait of Mother Idea
at the end of Part II, and also a ballet in which the Romans
pompously celebrate a triumph. The latter must certainly
have been staged by Hilverding.

Already a year before this event, the opera "Le Cinesi"
with a libretto by Metastasio was performed at the country
estate of Prince von Sachsen-Hildburghausen in Pressburg on
Sept. 24, 1754, as part of a rural festival to which the imperial
family had been invited. A fine description of the performance

comes from Dittersdorf. Since not only the imperial couple but a large number of court personnel were expected, a feast of immense proportions was prepared. Much of the ballet was to be presented by the prince's servants and peasants. A comic Caroussel, a Cuccagna, and a ballet were to be performed. 21 couples were selected for the ballet, and Angelo Pompeati, the husband of Theresa, was engaged. In order to train the peasants in the difficult routine, 40 members of the professional ballet had to work over them for three weeks.

Dittersdorf had composed a simple ballet melody, and on his advice the pastoral ballet was accompanied by bagpipes. It is worthwhile to read the description in Dittersdorf's autobiography; he is fascinated by the opera Gluck contributed to the occasion (see Paul Nettl, *Forgotten Musicians*): "It was not only the loveliness and brilliance of the introduction, occasionally accompanied by bells, triangles, small hand drums, and rattles, single or in ensemble, which charmed the audience. The music was a work of magic throughout."

This "Chinoiserie" was staged by the famous stage designer and architect Quaglio, and the four characters were given by some of Vienna's outstanding singers, Sivene by Theresa Heinisch, Tangia by Katharina Starzer, Silango by Joseph Friberth, and Lisinga by the famous Vittoria Tesi-Tramontini. The score, however, shows no indication of triangles or bells. Presumably these pseudo-Chinese instruments were improvised, as was the Chinese dance which followed the "azione teatrale." The score of this piece, also performed on April 17, 1755, at the Burgtheater, is entitled "Le Cinesi, componimento dramatico che introduce ad uno balle chinese."

Gluck's dramatic works can be grouped in two categories, 1) those which were composed for the repertory at large, that is, his full-length operas, and 2) those which were commissioned for particular events and thus have an improvisatory character, such as the little Chinese piece. Even in his later years Gluck had to undertake to deliver pieces for special festivities, among them "Parnasso confuso," which was performed at Schönbrunn on Jan. 27, 1765, with Archduke Leopold (later Emperor Leopold II) accompanying the entire score on the harpsichord, and with the older siblings of the family in the solo roles. The younger ones, among them Marie Antoinette, performed a Minuet, and one can see the charming performance which took place at the wedding of the future Emperor Joseph II and Maria Josepha of Bavaria on two contemporary portraits which Marie Antoinette ordered brought to Paris in 1778, and which are now housed in the Versailles museum.

Another court festival of Gluck's was "Le Feste d'Apollo," with a libretto by Frugoni, which stemmed from a commission for a stage work to be performed at Parma in 1769 for the wedding of the Infant Don Fernando of Spain and Archduchess Maria Amalia, who had participated in "Parnasso confuso" four years earlier. It consisted of three one-act pastorales with a prologue. The individual acts dealt with Philemon and Baucis, Aristeo, and finally "Orfeo" performed without breaks; in other words, a dramatic "Academy." After the symphony, the dancing began with a ballet movement taken from the opera "Telemacco," this type of borrowing being a common practice with Gluck. The autograph of the chorus "Del figlio d'Apollo" is in the possession of Dr. Hans Moldenhauer of Spokane, Washington, and affords some insight into the score. It is evident, for instance, that the chorus was followed by a dance and, indeed, the rhythms of "Del figlio" do have a dance-like character themselves.

In "Philemon and Baucis" there is a number entitled "Tempestà," but we dare not guess whether this superb piece of tone painting was used as the background of a dance.

As already indicated, the opera "Telemacco" (performed on Jan. 30, 1765) also contains dances. Its position is intermediate between Gluck's earliest operas and his reform operas. Khevenhüller notes that there was no ballet at the end of "Telemacco," which "shocked the spectators considerably." People were evidently not satisfied with single ballets; but the score contains only two pieces. Dittersdorf describes in detail another opera, "Il Trionfo di Clelia," with a libretto by Metastasio, which was performed on the second day of Pentecost in 1762 at Bologna. It too contained dances.

Among Gluck's ballets we must not forget to mention his last work, "Echo et Narcisse," which was produced by Elizabeth Duncan's school at the Munich court theater in 1913. But just as the "Magic Flute" is usually reckoned as Mozart's last work, "Iphigénie en Tauride" is Gluck's swan song. Mozart's "Titus" is neglected in favor of the "Magic Flute" and, similarly, Gluck's "Echo" is forgotten as his final work, probably because of the universal enthusiasm accorded "Iphigenie," and the general rejection of "Echo." The libretto of "Echo" is by the Swiss diplomat Theodor Baron Tschudi (born 1734) who, like Gluck's French librettist du Roullet, was interested in botany and agronomy.

The story of Echo and Narcissus comes from Ovid's *Metamorphoses*. It deals with the love of the nymph Echo for the beautiful shepherd Narcissus who does not respond to her, being preoccupied with his own beauty. The nymph, in her despair, turns into a mere voice which awakens only when it can answer a human sound from cave or ravine. Meanwhile, made aware of his egoism by Echo's death, Narcissus is turned into a flower and thus delivered from endless remorse.

The Neapolitan ambassador, Marchese Caraccioli, is said to have remarked: "Swiss words, German music, and French opera, these are three incompatible things." Everywhere the large number of dances was stressed, but only the appearance of the dancer Mlle. Théodore in the final ballet was praised, certainly because of Noverre's choreography. Gluck asserts that the ballets were completely unnecessary. In the journal "Memoires secrets," the composer's authorship of the ballets is even questioned, and the opera's editor in Gluck's complete works edition, Rudolf Gerber, declares that the final ballet is not the master's own work. A new version of the opera, sponsored largely by Tschudi, was unsuccessful. Gluck was so upset about the failure that he left Paris for ever on Oct. 7, shortly after the first performance (Sept. 21, 1779). Mlle. Théodore, mainstay of the ballets, was mentioned with praise in Melchior Grimm's "Correspondence littéraire." In the issue of February, 1779, he says: "The royal academy has been fortunate in engaging Mlle. Théodore. This young pupil of Monsieur Lany showed, in her debut, the unusual talent of a genre of dance all but forgotten; she seems to unite precision, nobility, and lightness in an extraordinary manner."

In the ballets, the dancers first appear in a Prologue, in which Amor's entourage (la suite d'amour) dances as a chorus. It is a charming Rococo piece for solo flute:

It is followed by "Air des peines," with oboe solo, a piece in binary form, whose melody is accompanied by spiccato in the second violins and violas. A short aria of Amor's is followed by an Andante in which two bassoons underscore a bizarre melody. The ensuing pantomime, which is the characterological representation of the following vocal portions sung by Amor, also uses a solo bassoon. Somewhat later the score again says, "on danse," to the accompaniment of a charming $^6/_8$ melody. The end of the prologue is a Contredanse in which a group of dancers surrounds Amor and leads him to a temple whose door closes after them. The introduction of this Contredanse is remarkable; it is the composer's bow to the Parisians, who were especially fond of that new dance.

In the drama itself we see Nayads and Sylvans singing and dancing. The ballet designated "Air pour les Nymphes et Sylvins" has phrases assigned to each of the two groups respectively, the nymphs as a rule being assigned to dance the higher passages. In the dances following, too, a graceful $^3/_8$ Minuet is done by the nymphs, a march-like "air marqué" in G minor by the Sylvans. Charming also is the pantomime in which Echo (Mlle. Théodore) lays down her sacrifice and the nymphs in her entourage wind garlands around the altar and set their baskets on its steps. Again a bassoon solo plays a serious C minor melody. The final dance consists of a hymn to Amor who, with his Zephyrs, ascends to the sky on a cloud. There follow a danced "Romance" in several movements, and a grand ballet of the kind used already in the days of the Ballet comique de la Reine in Paris.

DANCE IN THE REFORM OPERAS

While Gluck made dance an integral part of almost all his creations, it is the reform operas which constitute ballet's most important area. A year after the performance of "Don Juan," the opera "Orfeo ed Euridice" was staged on Oct. 5, 1762, at the Burgtheater. The libretto was, of course, by Calzabigi, who was, after all, largely responsible for Gluck's new concept of opera. This was Gluck's first application of French philosophy: unity and simplicity of plot, replacement of the recitativo secco by the accompagnato, and greater use of chorus and ballet. Indeed, the French ideal is most evident in the ballets, even though the Italian version of "Orfeo" did not go so far as the French one of 1774. In the latter, Act II contains the Finale of the "Don Juan" ballet, and the Gavotte which follows the flute solo is taken from "Paride ed Elena." Angiolini again created and directed the ballet, and the scenery was designed by Giovanni Maria Quaglio.

The score, printed in Paris by Chambon, says the following about the content of the dances: First ballet, shepherds and nymphs, Orfeo's entourage. In this ballet are presented the mourning rituals which the ancients performed at the gravesides of the dead: sacrifices, lighting incense, spreading flowers, pouring out wine and milk, dancing with sad mien, singing hymns of praise to the departed. Then youths, dressed as genii and carrying sacrificial gifts, chosen according to the wealth and position of the dead, are brought in. In this ballet, guardian spirits in the form of cupids weep at Euridice's urn; one of them, Hymen, extinguishes his torch as a symbol of the end of the marriage.

51

Second ballet: The spirits of the underworld try to frighten Orfeo. Third ballet: happy spirits in Elysium (the idea comes from Virgil, 6th book of the *Aeneid*). Fourth ballet: Heroes and heroines with Amor, Orfeo, and Euridice celebrate the wife's return and glorify the triumph of love. The torch of marriage, extinguished by Hymen in Act I, is now lit again by Amor with his own. Amor and Hymen exchange torches several times in the happy dance which ends the feast.

As a festival opera, "Orfeo" could not have a tragic ending, and Calzabigi, who himself had produced a happy end only under duress, was forced into conflict with Angiolini, who was convinced of the need for a tragic catastrophe for the sake of his ballets. It has been correctly pointed out that "Orfeo" does not develop through dialogue, but through tableaus. Unlike Caccini, Peri, and Monteverdi, Gluck does not describe the heroine's death, rather, he begins in the midst of the mourning rituals. A chorus of mourners is interrupted by Orfeo's cry, "Euridice!" According to the court painter Mannlich, who attended the Paris performance, Gluck instructed the singer to produce these cries truly as screams, as if his leg were being sawed off. Orfeo's deep sorrow appears somewhat transfigured in the first ballet in E flat major. It is as if he were regaining his composure after the first outpourings of grief, but after the tenth measure the unspeakable pain returns with a loud diminished seventh chord. The turn to the somber subdominant areas gives the pantomime an opportunity to show the whole range of pain and grief until, in the last few measures, the mood is calmer and there is again almost a kind of transfiguration.

The juxtaposition of inferno and Elysium in Act II is also expressed in unprecedented fashion in the pantomime. I am not sure whether it began already with the symphony and its threatening fanfares. The furies' chorus begins with the march-like rhythm ♩♩♩.♪♩ and is followed by a dance of the furies in C minor underscored by Orfeo's lyre. At the end of this scene the furies retire and the short Elysium-ballet follows, the piece used by Brahms for a set of piano variations. But it isn't feasible to speculate on the content of the dances. All of them have deep psychological meanings and make tremendous demands on choreographers.

In the second reform-opera, "Alceste," considered by some as the first genuine tragic opera, ballet also plays an important part. The significance ascribed to it by the master is evident from Gluck's manifesto which accompanies the engraved score of 1769. The libretto is lost, and we know little of the dance personnel at the first performance. Angiolini was in Russia but Noverre had been appointed in Vienna in 1767 and had found there a number of fine dancers. The theater log of 1772 gives us some of their names, and their characterization may be of interest here.

On p. 192 Mlle. Delphin is called "the most admirable subject so far found in Europe for the great and serious. Her dancing is virile; she performs her step with the utmost accuracy. Balance, sureness, and strength are hers. . . . Besides this amazing ability she has action, dignity, and expression, a pleasant arm, a good ear. Mlle. Vigano is a charming dancer. With a fill of expression she combines splendid execution. This is the danseuse Anacreontic; one can get an idea of her grace when one sees her dance. Her expression is always sensitive. She knows the art of making spectators feel all the passions which she represents, and she imparts to them grace and truthfulness alike."

Among the male dancers, Simonet is named first (p. 197): "Herr Simonet, large of stature, dances the serious genre. He is strong, sure, knows how to use speed and inertia to advantage. He possesses great powers of balance, his movements are gentle and graceful."

Calzabigi's libretto of "Alceste" is only partially based on Euripides' "Alkestis." It has the inevitable "fine lieto." All of Euripides's crassness and realism are gone, especially the Hercules scenes. In Calzabigi's version, Apollo is the deus ex machina who accomplishes the return of Alkestis as a token of thanks to her husband Admetos. In the French version, which was performed in Paris on April 23, 1776, Gluck took several pieces from his earlier works, e.g., the flute solo in the Divertissement of the last act, which comes from the middle movement of the overture "L'innocenza giustificata."

Much has been written about the differences between the French and Italian versions, especially that Gluck introduced Hercules as Alceste's savior in Paris, basically interfering with the rule of the gods. It has also been said that the French version emphasizes dramatic contrast, and the celebration for Admetos' recovery bears out that statement. Gluck stressed it on the advice of Rousseau. Consequently Act II did not begin with a continuation of the mourning in Act I, but a great scene of recovery was constructed: "Que les plus doux transports succèdent aux alarmes." After the chorus appears a grand ballet, called Passacaille, but hardly related to that old dance form. The G minor Andante is interesting, for it is a Polonaise with the proper Polish rhythm. In such a mass score there must have been little room for expressive dance, but the short pantomime in C minor which precedes the oracle scene allows the listener to sense the choreographer's art in its sobbing phrases on the diminished seventh, with the Lombard rhythms.

The French version's ballet is generally more expansive than the Italian. A ballet of large dimensions closes the opera; it consists of an Andante, a march, and the famous A major Andante beloved by generations. There follow a broad French Minuet, a Gavotte, and the inevitable Chaconne.

A year after the first performance of "Alceste" on Sept. 23, 1777, Gluck's "Armide," after an old text by Quinault, was performed. The story of the sorceress-queen of Damascus falling in love with the crusader hero Rinaldo, who remains cool to her, is the substance of the plot, in which love and hate alternate and the scale of human passions is unfolded. The opera has been described as a combination of Italian and French art, the statically decorative dance tableaus balanced by dramatic action. In Act IV we are reminded of the flower-maiden scene in "Parsifal." The ballet (Chaconne) in Act V takes our thoughts to the Venusberg bachanale, but it does not approach Wagner's powerful effects. The furies' dance in Act III invites comparison with those of "Don Juan" and "Orfeo." Here it is the octave leaps and the soaring 32nd notes in unison which grip the audience and set the choreographer a difficult task. Compared with the others, this furies' dance is rather a piece of tone painting. The beautiful Sicilienne in G minor in the last act, however, is entirely taken from "Don Juan."

One of Gluck's and Noverre's greatest inspirations was "Paride ed Elena," performed on Nov. 30, 1770, at the Kärntnertortheater. Again the libretto was by Calzabigi. The authors may have been attracted by the ethnological aspects of the plot, for Phrygian and Spartan cultures are juxtaposed. Paris is the sensitive, pining singer who in Acts III and IV is possessed by consuming passions expressed through demoniac tones worthy of Beethoven. Elena, according to Gluck's preface, is styled a primitive character with corresponding simplicity of melody and harmony, until she falls in love with her abductor. The stylistic contrast of recitative (Spartan) and arioso (Phrygian) symbolizes the two cultures, and this contrast is underscored by ballets and choruses.

Thus we see a rose garden before the gates of Sparta and a Trojan sacrifice to Venus so that she will honor her promise that Paris, in return for his decision in her favor, should possess the world's most beautiful woman. The prince watches the sacrifice and sings three long arias whose continuation is a dance. In a charming aria in B flat the doves of Venus are tenderly praised, and the second stanza is played by the oboe as an accompaniment to dance. Then Erasto-Amor approaches with his Spartan entourage, whose angular melodies, says Moser, show their origin with the stern Lycurgus. The dances which now follow, closing Act I, graphically express the contrast between the two peoples, for example, the Spartan C minor dance with its unison passages, the F major Maëstoso, likewise beginning with an Unisono using triadic melodies and closing in Turkish style, as well as the F major Allegro. The dulcet C major piece and the Amabile moderato in B flat, which is reminiscent of the dance of the spirits in "Orfeo," are intended to sound Phrygian. The angular, dotted, melody of the athletes' ballet in Act III is music for a genuine Olympiad, a dance which presumably showed all sorts of ancient sport. The athletes appear again, this time in a C major Maëstoso, a march followed by a Chaconne, and again by Gluck's favorite Gavotte, which Brahms later arranged for Clara Schumann. The end of Act V contains first an F major dance, then a series of choruses in which the happy couple revel on a nocturnal lake and in a Mediterranean landscape. There is an anecdote, printed in the "Journal de Paris" of 1788, in which Gluck pointed out the anachronism of showing the Spartans as an austere people long before the laws of Lycurgus. As a matter of fact, the triumvirate of Gluck, Calzabigi, and Noverre were concerned primarily with producing dramatic contrasts.

The significance which Gluck ascribed to the ballet is evident from a report by J. F. Reichardt about a Vienna performance of one of his operas. The scenery for the first ballet caught fire. Much commotion ensued, dancers and spectators tried to save themselves. Meanwhile the fire was quelled and Act II was about to begin. Gluck, however, demanded a repetition of the Act I ballet. Argument turned into a quarrel, the female performers trembled with fright, the men had already undressed. Gluck finally climbed on a chair and called across the theater, in the presence of the imperial family: "Either the ballet will be repeated or the opera is over for tonight." The ballet had to be begun again, and the performance concluded successfully.

Pas de Quatre with Marie Sallé; after Lancret (Foto: Archiv Balcar)

"El Zapateado" (Foto: Archiv Balcar)

GLUCK'S SWAN SONG

Gluck had most probably met the "Bailli" (commander of the Maltese order) Le Blanc du Roullet (1716-1786) in Rome in 1756 at a performance of "Antigono," and had met him again in Vienna as attaché to the French embassy. It was du Roullet's ambition to bring the master to Paris, but he was also very interested in writing a libretto for the reformer of opera. And so he recast Racine's "Iphigénie en Aulide" as an opera which Gluck composed immediately and played for the visiting Charles Burney in 1772. In an open letter written on Aug. 1, 1772 to A. d'Auvergne, a director of the Paris opera, du Roullet describes the work with enthusiasm and asks whether Paris would be interested in it. Gluck himself wrote to the "Mercure de France" about a combination of French and Italian styles and proposed the creation of a kind of international music, thereby abolishing "the ridiculous differences among national styles." He is thinking, he said, of his "mature style" in which the Italians' pure melodic line was to be replaced by a rhythmically declamatory kind of speech. Gluck cited Rousseau who would have helped and advised him.

After examining the first act, d'Auvergne declared himself ready to perform "Iphigénie" since it surpassed all other operas, on condition that Gluck agree to furnish six operas in this style. Evidently d'Auvergne, tiring of the Rameau style, had a vague intention of sponsoring a change in French opera. When delays threatened, Marie Antoinette, a former pupil of the master's and now the Dauphine, simply ordered the performance and Gluck was asked to come to Paris, which he did in November of 1773.

Ballet had been put in the foreground too vigorously in Paris. Grimm sneers in his "Correspondance littéraire:" "French opera is a kind of drama in which the fate of all characters is to see everyone dancing around." And in his *Petit Prophèt de Boehmisch Broda* he relates that he went to opera and was terribly bored by a collection of Minuets, arias, Gavottes, Tambourins, and Contredanses, which continued for 2½ hours, and that the dancers described the arias while the singers sang them, their steps slavishly accompanying every eighth-note. "People call it a festival," he wrote, "even though it was no such thing, but rather a joyless piece of acting. It simply would not end, though the dancers made bored faces, thereby confusing the singers." An so on in this satirical vein.

Rousseau too says that "there is an art to placing ballets in an opera." If a prince is happy, people dance for joy; if he is sad, they dance to relieve his grief. Everything in life is danced: priests, soldiers, even devils dance to the grave, everybody dances about everything. Under the philosopher's pressure people tried to find a new style, and Gluck, even though a German, was just the man to create a new French style, as the Italian Lully had created the Théâtre lyrique. Rousseau had even sent Gluck a note after the dress rehearsal, saying "You have indeed accomplished what I had thought impossible." Of course the "citizen of Geneva" had always considered French music completely unsuitable. But if we remember that Gluck in this opera relied more than ever on his own earlier works, imbuing them with Italian spirit, we must admit that the Gallicizing power which contemporaries saw in "Iphigénie en Aulide" was more or less a pipe dream.

Euripides already had divided his piece into two parts, and most librettists followed his example. In our case, du Roullet, according to Grimm, had dealt ill with the noblest of French plays and had committed depredations on Racine's masterpiece. But the "arbiter elegantiarum" of Paris did admit that Gluck's music furnished the most moving spots with a gentility and sensitivity which covered the libretto's weaknesses.

To be sure, the French are the great masters of ballet, but who does not remember the tragicomic incidents at the first performance of "Tannhäuser" in Paris in 1861? Gluck, however, not only wished to oblige the Parisians, he actually needed the ballet as a dramatic medium, having built "Iphigénie" into a dramatic work of immense format which consists of an inner as well as an outer plot and has need of a wide sphere of activity: splendid and pompous entrances for contrasting the differences between the heroic (Achilles), the ceremonial (Calchas), the proud and demoniac (Clytemnestra), agony of the soul (Agamemnon), youthful loveliness (Iphigénie). Gluck once said that theater is not big enough to hold "Iphigénie en Aulide" considering the choruses and ballets. His choreographic advisors were the elder Vestris as well as the dancers who appeared, Gardel, Léger, LePicq, and, among the ladies, Allard, Peslin, Guimard, and Heinel. Dauberval too was outstanding among the choreographers. In 1776 the ballet's ensemble counted 109 members and was increased to 148 the following year.

As already mentioned Gluck took much of "Iphigénie" from earlier works. Thus the ballet movement in Act II is the overture to the "Don Juan" ballet, which is also the source of three ballet movements in the Divertissement of Act I. The Passacaille in Act II comes from "Paride ed Elena," as does the Divertissement from Act III, while the ballet movement No. 2 in Act I comes from "Alessandro." The graceful Minuet in Act II is already present in "La rencontre imprévue" and comes from "Trionfo di Clelia." When Einstein says that the orchestra here speaks for the first time, evoking images which words cannot express and which stir the soul's subconscious, he is speaking primarily of the ballet movements which have a degree of musical intensity obscuring all previous ballet music.

Gluck's swan song is his most monumental work, "Iphigenie en Tauride," whose grandiose concept is worthy of Sophocles. Goethe was greatly impressed by this music drama, saying it was "devilishly human." But the old Hellenic concept of fate is present, the "noble simplicity and silent grandeur" contrasted with a spiteful world notwithstanding. Perhaps "Iphigenie en Tauride" is Gluck's best libretto, written as it was by du Roullet's young protegé Nicolas François Guillard. It was produced in Gluck's presence on May 18, 1779, with undeniable success. Let us point out that "Iphigenie en Tauride" was the only opera before Pfitzner's "Palestrina" in which love between man and woman played no part. A group of dances, coupled with grandiose choral scenes, present the metaphysical and cultural background. The barbaric Scythian dance in Scene 3, with its bass drum, cymbals, triangle, piccolo, and unison passages is unparalleled in music literature, and we can imagine that the choreographer of the day had to master all arts of expression. The chorus itself dances and recites in starkly ancient fashion.

The pantomime in Act II, by Orestes and the furies, is of great significance: the Eumenides appear from upstage and surround Orestes. Some of them perform a horror-ballet around him, the others speak to him intensively. But Orestes is unconscious, a fine decision of the librettist's who, in this work, always projects the characters' suffering on the audience. This Eumenide-ballet is taken from a similar scene in Gluck's ballet "Semiramis." The long tradition of horror scenes, based on 17th century Venetian opera, here comes to a climax. The manner in which the Eumenides encircle the sleeping Orestes, terrifying him with the likeness of his murdered mother so that he cries out repeatedly and finally, at the climax, tear him from his sleep so that, horrified, he mistakes Iphigénie for his own mother, is so powerful that the scene can hardly be described with words. In the final act we again find music taken from "Semiramis."

"Iphigenie en Tauride" is undeniably the climax of Gluck's career, in spite, or perhaps because, of its being a product of his old age, a final integration of his entire dramatic experience.

And just as it is the climax of his operatic creation it also represents the high point of tragic ballet in the service of Gluck's Gesamtkunstwerk.

MOZART

In contrast to Beethoven and Johann Strauss, who never learned how to dance, Mozart was an excellent and passionate dancer. He was not only an enthusiastic billiard player and very fond of games, but also a clever master of ceremonies and an amateur choreographer. He loved to dance the minuet and, according to his biographer, Nissen, never missed the *redoutes* (Public masked balls) that were held in theaters and private dances given by his friends. He may have been a pupil of Vestris, and in any case, "he danced and wrote pantomimes and ballets. In *redoutes* he often wore character masks and was inimitable as a Harlequin and Pierrot." On January 22, 1783, Mozart wrote to his father from Vienna: "I gave a ball last week in my apartment, but of course the gentlemen each paid two gulden; we started at 6 p.m, and stopped at 7—what? only one hour?—no, no, at 7 in the morning! You won't understand that I had enough space. [He had just moved to Baron Wetzlar, a rich Jew]. I have a room 1000 steps long and I step wide, and a bedroom, a foyer, and beautiful large kitchen; and adjoining our rooms there are two more beautiful large ones which are still empty—those I used for our dance. Baron and Baroness Wetzlar were also present, as was Baroness Waldstaedten, Herr von Edelbach, Gilowsky the windbag, young Stephanie *et uxor*, Adamberger and his wife, the Langes, etc." In the same letter he wrote: "You doubtlessly know that this is Carnival time and that people here dance quite as much as in Salzburg and Munich; so I should like to go disguised as Harlequin (without anyone knowing about it) because there are so many Jackasses at these masked balls. Please send me your Harlequin costume, but it would have to be very soon—for we won't attend *redoutes* until I get it; they are in full swing, but we prefer private balls. . ." "On Shrove Monday (March 3)," he wrote on March 12, "our company of masks went to the *redoute* and performed a pantomime during the half hour intermission between the dances. My sister-in-law was Columbine, I was Harlequin, my brother-in-law was Pierrot, and old dancing master (Merk) was Pantaloon, a painter (Grassi) was the dottore. Both plot and music were by me. Dancing-master Merk was kind enough to coach us, and I must say we really acted quite well. I am enclosing the program which was distributed by someone dressed as a courier. The verses, even if they are only doggerels, could be better; I did not write them—the actor, Mueller, dashed them off."

The actor, Johann Henrich Mueller (1738-1815), whose original name is said to have been Schroeder, was born in Halberstadt, studied at the universities of his native town and Halle, but joined the Schuchs' theatrical company in 1775. This was the first step toward his remarkable career in the theater, which was climaxed by a commission from Emperor Joseph II, in 1776, to travel through Germany and find outstanding actors for the newly-founded National Theater.

But let us return from Mueller, librettist of Mozart's masquerade, to Mozart's dance entertainment. It is easy to recognize that it did not merely consist of social dancing, but that entire pantomimes were performed. In Mozart's Collected Works, Series XXIV, No. 18, there is a fragment of a violin part from this masquerade in which Pantaloon, Colombine, dottore and other characters of comedia dell'arte participate.

In the pantomime, Pantaloon and Colombine quarrel. Pantaloon is the good, old, candid Venetian merchant, always in love, always cheated by rival, manservant or maid. Dottore appears, the braggadocio who, as a Professor of the University of Bologna, talks the greatest possible nonsense under the cloak of profound wisdom. Pantaloon treats him ceremoniously and introduces him to Colombine as her potential husband. Colombine is sad even though Pantaloon tries to humor her. Mozart's

Pantaloon, Pierrot and Dottore lie on the ground, and show. This is a longer pantomime involving a change of tempo; the quarrel between the latter two is well characterized by staccato octaves. Then, on Pantaloon's instructions, a small table is supposed to be moved, but Pierrot pretends to be too weak. In the following scene in which Dottore kneels down in front of Colombine, Pantaloon and Pierrot bring the table, to the sounds of this melody:

The next melody, which expressed Colombine's sadness, causes us to regret that Mozart did not finish the Pantomime. There follows a scene in which Harlequin looks out of a peep music adapts itself to her changing moods. Pierrot rushes in. a Turk appears suddenly in a larghetto "alla Turca" (which, however, was not Mozart's own designation). The last remarks in the fragment merely say that Pierrot is afraid of the dead Harlequin (adagio) but regains his courage (risoluto). What the rest of the pantomime was to have been cannot be ascertained.

FRENCH BALLET

The ballet plays a tremendous part in the entire history of opera. The *Ballet de la Reine* is considered the starting point. It was performed for the first time in 1573, as *Ballet de la Reine Cathérine de Medici en l'honneur des ambassadeurs de Pologne* (Ballet of the Queen Catherine de Medici, in honor of the ambassadors of Poland). This world-famous performance took place under the influence of reform ideas, especially those of Jean-Antoine de Baïf, founder of the *Academie de Musique et de Poesie* (1571) which glorified the blending of the arts in the sense of the Wagnerian *Gesamtkunstwerk*. This was the origin of the *Ballet de Cour*, which consisted of the following parts: 1. *L'ouverture* (Overture—exposition of the piece through recitation or singing); 2. *Les entrées* (succession of scenes; no more than five are required) ; 3. *Le grand ballet* (the entire ensemble appearing in the final dance).

Gluck and Mozart still used the Chaconne as a final grand ballet, the choreographic climax of the opera. All the great French poets—among them Corneille, Malherbe, Bois-Robert, Sorel—had contributed to this form which had reached its peak with Lully and Rameau. A simplified form of the *Ballet de Cour* was the *Ballet-Masquerade* which dated to the early 17th century and featured grotesque disguises. Less spectacular and expensive were private performances in which members of Court and nobility participated. How grotesque they now appear to us, those *Ballets de Matronnes, Ballets de Singes,* and *Ballets de Bouteilles*!

Another variant of the *Ballet de Cour* is the *Ballet à Entree*, in which the appearance of individual groups is announced by singing or recitation.

In France the *Ballet de Cour* was an independent art form and a preliminary to opera; in Italy it was closely linked with it. In the 16th century *Mauresques*—originally representations of battles between Moors and Christians in the Middle Ages— became ballet intermezzi, such as triumphal marches and processions. This applies to the *Mauresques* in Cavalieri's *Rappresentazione di anima e di corpo* (1600) and Monteverdi's *Orfeo* (1607). In his treatise *Practica di fabricar scene* (1639), Sabbatini calls all pantomimes simply Mauresques.

The relationship between France and Italy in this field was reciprocal. Monteverdi, who had stayed in France with Gonzaga, published a suitelike ballet, in his *Scherzi Musicali* (1607). His *Ballo Delle Ingrate,* also arranged like a suite, was performed a year later.

When opera was transplanted from Italy to Germany, it was first of all in Vienna that Italian, French and native elements were combined. The choreographer, Beccaria, a pupil of Cesare Negri, became dancing-master at the court of Rudolph II. Among his successors at the Austrian Court were Santo and Domenico Ventura, father and son who cultivated the Italian ballet methods under Ferdinand III and Leopold I.

Lully, in Paris, composed the dances for his own operas with painstaking attention for the subject-matter treating the ballet as a form of primary importance; but in Vienna the dances in the operas of Bertali, Cesti, Draghi, Ziani, Badia, Caldara, etc. were written by native composers such as Wolfgang Ebner; Johann Heinrich Schmelzer and his son, Andreas Anton Schmelzer; Johann Joseph Hoffer; and his successor, Nicola Matteis, an Italian living in England, who worked in Vienna around 1700. Johann Heinrich Schmelzer (died 1680) was instrumental in introducing popular elements into Viennese ballets and into art music as a whole. Besides the numerous Italian and French dances of the time, those written as suites served as dance intermezzi between acts and at the end of the opera, as well as in the dance divertissements (corresponding to the *French Ballets à entrées*). They included dances such as Galliards, Allemands, Courants, Sarabandes, Gigues, Trezzas, Rigaudons, Branles, Traccanarios, Menuets, Gavottes, Bourees, Passepieds, Bergamasks, Canaries, Chaconnes, Passacaglias. Certain dances are designated simply as *Arie* or as *Arie Viennesi*. They are dances in ¾ time and with alpine triadic elements that turn out to be typical Austrian Ländler and early German waltzes. One of these first original waltzes, a choral waltz from a ballet *Singspiel* performed in 1660, was discovered and published by this author. The degree to which Vienna depended on France as early as in the days of Leopold I can be seen from the fact that the manuscripts preserved in the form of sketches at the National Library, and in the full score at the St. Mauriz Archives at Kremsier, Moravia, include *Balletti Francesi di aula Regia di Francia*—dances in the style of Lully. These dances seem to have been performed at the house of the French ambassador in Vienna, Grenonville, according to the correspondence of Leopold I with his Spanish ambassador, Poetting. Due to the French influence, there also exist numerous *Introduzioni di balletti*, counterparts to the French court ballets. But in contrast to Louis XIV, who appeared on the stage as Jupiter and was glorified by his courtiers acting as extras, Leopold I never appeared as a dancer. He was satisfied to be known as a composer of ballets, and numerous dances, which he wrote in the style of Schmelzer, preserved in Vienna and Kremsier. The development of the military ballet at the Austrian Court also reflects the Emperor's personality.

At the Austrian Court, the two Venturas were succeeded by the Frenchman, Alexandre Philibois, and after him came Franz Hilverding von Weven (1710-1768). The latter devoted himself to perfecting the choreographic detail of the pantomime. Occasionally, he used tragic plots, thus initiating the tragic ballet pantomime. At the Court of Louis XIV, the choreographer, Duprés, even at the age of sixty enchanted his contemporaries, among them Casanova, with his harmonic dance

67

sequences and his magnificent appearance. He was the teacher of Gaetano Vestris (1729-1808) and Jean-George Noverre (1727-1810). Noverre defended his tragic ballet pantomimes in his *Lettres sur la dance et les ballets* in 1760, and is credited with having reformed the ballet. A large number of his ballets became famous, mainly because of their scores composed by Francois Granier of Lyon; Florian Deller and Johann Joseph Rudolph, of Stuttgart, and Joseph Starzer and Franz Asplmayer of Vienna.

As early as 1767, during his visit to Vienna, Mozart was impressed by the dances of the famous Florentinian, Gaetano Vestris (see Leopold Mozart's letter to Hagenauer, September 29). He saw some ballets for an opera by Hasse, with Vestris' choreography and, according to Nissen, took dancing lessons with him. Vestris was the teacher of Jean-George Noverre, who had been engaged as balletmaster for Vienna by the impresario and notorious adventurer, Giuseppe Afflisio (1719-1787), a friend of Casanova's and manager of the Kärntnerthortheater. In this capacity, Noverre made his debut on September 10, in the machine and pantomime ballet *L'Apotheose d'Hercule* with Vestris appearing as a guest. The Mozarts arrived in Vienna but four days later and, therefore, missed this memorable ballet performance. They also missed the performance of Gluck's *Alceste* on December 26, with a ballet contributed by Noverre— *dans le gout grotesque*— for the family were staying at Bruenn, Moravia, at the time, scared away from Vienna by a smallpox epidemic. Still, we may assume that Mozart did meet Noverre at about that time and attended some rehearsals and performances by the great master of classical ballet. Their collaboration, however, started much later, in Italy. It is doubtful that Noverre actually was the choreographer of Mozart's *Azione teatrale: Ascanio in Alba* (K. 111) as Erich Schenk tells us in his excellent book *Wolfgang Amadeus Mozart* (Vienna, 1955, P. 268), for in a letter to his wife, dated September 13, 1771, Leopold explicitly mentions the balletmasters, Le Picq and Jean Favier.

When the Archbishop of Salzburg, Hieronymus Colloredo, went to Vienna in the summer of 1773, Leopold decided to follow him with his son. Young Mozart had accumulated so much experience and fame during his travels to Italy, whence he had just returned, that he could consider himself eligible for a position at Court. Secretly, he thought of the position of the ailing conductor, Florian Leopold Gassmann, who actually died a year later; but this went to the Court Composer Bonno. We may assume that Mozart's many vague plans included a ballet, especially since Noverre was then earning laurels in the Austrian capital. At any rate, we know that the Mozarts dined at Noverre's on August 29, no doubt because Leopold was hoping for a ballet commission for Wolfgang. However, the Mozarts, who returned to Salzburg on September 26, could hardly have attended the performance of Noverre's ballet satire on Gasparo Angiolini, his great rival. Neither did they see the performance, on January 6, 1774, of Noverre's ballet, *Les Horaces et les Curiaces*, with music by Starzer. When Mozart stayed in Mannheim in 1777, he saw a number of ballets created by the Parisian, Etienne Lauchery. Lauchery was director of Court balls and of the Dance Academy, and his composers were Toeschi and Cannabich. Mozart mentions him in a letter to his father of December 3, 1777, presumably as a travel companion to Paris, together with flutist, Wendling, and oboist, Ramm. At any rate, he also seems to have been a composer for Leopold writes on December 11, "I saw some duets for two violins by Sgr. Lauchery, *Danseur de S:A:SS: l'Electeurs,* at Robini Sigerl's." In 1778, when Mozart was in Paris with his mother, he renewed the acquaintance with Noverre. On April 5, Wolfgang wrote to his father that he could dine at Noverre's as often as he wanted and that the balletmaster was trying to find a spot for an opera to be composed by Mozart, the libretto of which was completed up to the second act. On May 14, he again mentioned to his father that he would soon receive the libretto, but would have to submit it first to the General Administrator of the *Académie Royale de Musique*. In his optimism, he did not doubt that M. de Vismes, the opera director who owed his position to Noverre, would accept it. He also believed that Noverre would soon stage a new ballet and that Mozart would compose the music. Soon thereafter, however, he mentions his friendship with the famous ballet composer and horn virtuoso, Johann Joseph Rudolph (Rodolphe) who was then working in Paris. In his biography, Schenk correctly points out that Noverre had great difficulties there. His former pupil, Queen Marie-Antoinette, had appointed him to the Grand Opera at a salary of 12,000 francs. She had also appointed him manager of her festivities at the Petit Trianon, and within a year he had increased the dance personnel from 109 to 148 members. The source of information on Noverre's difficulties in Paris is a letter of Mme. Gardel to Marquis Amazaga, which Grimm reprinted in the August 1776 edition of his *Correspondence Littéraire*: "Not even you, my old friend in good times and bad, would expect to hear what I am going to tell you. Who would doubt that Gardel, working at the Opera for 19 years, admired for his great talent and for the devotion to his duties, for his charm and his honesty (I have sacrificed 20,000 Pounds for his training), has become famous. Now some administrators come to the Queen and induce her to appoint a stranger who had tried at least twenty times to get into the Opera, always without success. Forgotten is the dancing master of the Queen, the ballet master of the Court, the darling of the audience, beloved by his associates, who for 6 years has been producing the most beautiful ballets in the world. One still remembers *Erlinde*, which he staged for the Court and which represented a siege. The Comtesse de Noailles graciously told me that the marshals of France had asked where Gardel had studied military strategy, that the dauphin had dreamed about it all night, and many other pleasant things on the subject, and this man should now be treated like a student! One has dared to subordinate to Noverre the man who is called the famous Gardel in England and everywhere else! My son is kind, modest and honest, but he would be a charlatan if one did this to him!

"Said Noverre arrives with one of those letters of recommendation one sends along like a dispatch note, from the Empress to the Queen, who tells the theater managers that it would be agreeable to her if the bearer would produce some ballets, if it would cause no trouble; divine words, indeed, indicating the kindness and generosity of her soul! Her Majesty and the Empress cannot know that the position of the ballet master at the Paris Opera, like that of President, is hereditary and automatically goes to the first dancer. No stranger has a right to it unless the ballet master resigns, like M. Dupré.

"But my son does not feel like renouncing his rights and being subordinated to a master from the provinces, and from Germany. Usually these gentlemen come to Paris in order to study—not to teach the great teachers. Little Noverre is just slightly too ambitious. When he presented himself 30 years ago, he was sent to the Fair to perform his Chinese ballets. . . . Forgive me Marquis, for boring you with these things; I am as modest as my son as long as I am treated fairly; but when I feel humiliated, I rise like a cedar."

Madame Gardel (Gardella) was one of those ladies of the ballet who comes in for some sharp comment in Casanova's memoirs. The Venetian adventurer reported that as a young girl she was the mistress of his Venetian benefactor, Malipiero. His other mistress was the younger Theresa Imer, who later became famous as the Pompeati, the primadonna and "entrepreneuse" of the Bach-Abel concerts in London. Gardella was three years younger than Casanova and her face had, as he writes, "a charming expression of cuteness." According to Casanova, Gardella later held a glamorous position in Stuttgart under the name of Augusta, and in 1757, was acknowledged as the favorite mistress of Duke Karl Eugen of Württemberg. Her husband was the dancer, Michele de l'Agata, who took poison shortly after her death. After he had escaped the lead chambers, Casanova met Gardella again in Munich. When he came to Stuttgart, he was invited to a magnificent meal; through the dinner conversation we learn that Gardella's aunt was a fat, blind woman, a beggar on a bridge in Venice. Casanova ends his many lascivious remarks about the dancer with the statement that she danced in Stuttgart under Noverre or apparently misused her power over the Duke against the great ballet master. This would explain the wrath of the aging ex-ballerina against the "stranger Noverre."

Leopold Mozart overestimated Noverre's power when he informed his son on March 16 that the Pope had bestowed upon him the Order of the Golden Spur. On April 20, 1778, he sent his regards to Grimm, Mme. Epinay, Gossec, Wendling and Raff, and also to Noverre and his wife. Discussing Wolfgang's French opera project, he suggests, in a long letter, dated April 29, that Wolfgang go over the words with Grimm and Noverre, and later, on May 28, to consult Noverre about the "expression of emotion." This means that Wolfgang should adapt his music to the style of movement of the French—a formidable task where Leopold even may have overestimated his son's scope. Leopold corresponded with Noverre, as we can see in his letter of August 13. Leopold liked to quote French letters and so he copied a passage from Noverre's: "You see, dear master, that in a country where so many mediocre and miserable people have made vast fortunes, I am afraid that it will not be easy for your son . . . I have faithfully informed you about this not in order to make you sad, but so that together we can make the best of it. It is regrettable that the death of the Elector of Bavaria has prevented your son from getting a position in Mannheim." On the other hand, Leopold mentioned on August 27, that he would have written to Noverre long before had he known his title and his address. At any rate, Noverre was extremely friendly toward Wolfgang; perhaps friendlier than Grimm. Mozart's mother wrote on April 5 to Leopold: "He can dine daily at Noverre's and also at Madame Depine (Epinay). . . ."

Unlike Grimm, Noverre never lost Wolfgang's friendship. On September 12, he wrote from Vienna: "The ballet master, Antoine, was brought here from Munich—and they are looking all over Vienna and the suburbs for dancers—because there is a sad reminder of Noverre's still around; but since they have not moved a leg in eight years, most of them are as stiff as sticks." The friendship with Noverre produced one lasting result: the ballet *Les petits riens*. Jahn thinks that, for the sake of this ballet, Noverre kept making promises to Mozart and raising hopes about an opera. But, as Abert remarked, there is no reason to accuse Noverre of such perfidy. Artistic politics in Paris were stronger than the influence of Noverre and even of De Vismes, the manager, whose business with French operas had been bad. The music of the French ballet enchants us still. According to the letter of May 14, Leopold Mozart had inquired about the ballet and Wolfgang had answered: "About the ballet of Noverre, I never wrote anything except that he might do another one, he just needed half a ballet and I am writing the music for it—that is, six pieces of other composers will be in it, all miserable old French arias. I'll have written the symphony and the Contre dance—12 pieces all told. This ballet was performed four times already, with the greatest success—but now I absolutely do not want to do anything if I don't know in advance how much I can get, because this one was done out of friendship for Noverre." On June 11, the playbill of the Grand Opera announced the performance of Piccini's opera buffa, *Les fausses jumelles*, or *Le finte gemelle*, and the ballet pantomime, *Les petits riens,* by Mr. Noverre. The composer, Mozart, is not mentioned and his friend, Baron Grimm, did not bother to say one word about the charming music of his former protegé.

The *Journal de Paris* of June 12, reported about the play as follows: "It consists of three separate episodes. The first, is purely Anacreontic: Amor has been caught in a net and put into a cage; the composition is very lovely. Miss Guimard and the young Mr. Vestris deplore all graces whose intentions are unmistakable. The second is the play by Colin-Maillard; Mr. Auberval, whose talent rates high in public favor, has the main part. In the third, Amor teases two shepherdesses by introducing another shepherdess dressed as a shepherd. Miss Asselin has the part of the shepherd and the Misses Guimard and Allard are the shepherdesses. The two shepherdesses fall in love with the alleged shepherd who, in order to clear up the misunderstanding, shows them "his" bosom. The intelligence and gracefulness of the three famous dancers make this scene rather risque. We noticed that several voices called "bis" at the moment where Mlle. Asselin enlightens the two shepherdesses. The various figures which end the ballet had much applause." It might be useful here to quote Grimm's review in *Correspondence Littéraire*: "The performance of *Finte Gemelle* (by Piccini) was followed by a new ballet pantomime by Mr. Noverre, *Les petits riens*. It consists of episode scenes; a succession of unconnected tableaux worthy of the Muse of Anacreon or of the brush of a Boucher or a Watteau. The nature of love as personified by Madame Guimard and the roguish play of her partner, Monsieur D' Auberval, deserve much applause. One followed with great interest the tricks of Amor who brings a new companion to the two shepherdesses, Guimard and Allard, who, however, hides a charming girl under the shepherd's mask. The actions of these three characters develop into three clever and charming scenes. However, at a certain moment in the last scene, a murmur of dissent inevitably mixes with the applause, for the moral standards of our theaters are very high. We are referring to the moment when the alleged shepherd, defending himself against the two shepherdesses who vie for his favors, ends the game once and for all by revealing his (her) sex. However, Mlle. Asselin modestly and gracefully manages to restrain her partners, this pantomime always splits the audience into two camps. And the voices calling "bis" cannot fail to hear the objections of the others."

The charming music hibernated for 100 years in the library of the Paris Opera until Victor Wilder in 1872 brought it back to life. Besides the overture, Mozart wrote some free movements, a pantomime, two gavottes and a passepied. No. 9, the *Gavotte joyeuse*, appeared in part in the Violin Concerto (K.271a) in D, whose authorship had been considered doubtful until Wilder's discovery established the connection of its finale with the Parisian ballet. In the 6th gavotte, Mozart used a Czech folksong, "Let us go to Bethlehem," which appears in Jaromir Erben's collection of folksongs.

After the success of *Les petits riens,* Mozart wrote another ballet for the Grand Opera. Only sketches have been preserved, which are kept at the *Bibliotheque Nationale* in Paris. Mozart's manuscript contains his own stage directions concerning a blacksmith and his wife (*Le forgeron travaille*).

To an appealing theme Mozart makes a remark, in poor French, the sense of which is not quite clear: Apparently the plot revolves around the blacksmith who does not see his wife and dances with another woman. Another remark reveals that the wife returns and the other woman runs away. The blacksmith faints and she must follow him. She orders him to go down on his knees before her; first he refuses, then obeys, and she demands that he kiss her hand. They dance a gigue.

I have published a piano score of the sketches to the lost ballet, in "W. A. Mozart, 1756-1791" (S. Fischer).

As we can see from the *Petits riens,* not even Noverre could carry out his ideas of the dramatic ballet. In his famous *Lettres sur la Dance,* the great choreographer calls this kind of work, "Divertissement de Dance," and Mozart's ballet actually differs greatly from the great scene for ballet and orchestra, in works by Florian Deller, Rudolph, Starzer and in Gluck's *Don Juan.* The most important part is the overture; it's a rich instrumentation with its thematic use of the wind instruments showing the Mannheim influence. It seems that Mozart has adjusted the structure of his ballets to the taste of the French, which he despised, for not even the charming second theme appears in the dominant as would have been customary. In Germany or Italy, Mozart would have called this introduction *Intrada.* Abert points to a similarity with the first air of Susanna in *Figaro,* which derives from Paisiello, and he mentions the ingenuity with which the numerous ideas are transposed, varied and punctuated with new material, like the overtures to French comic operas. The dances are in two parts, in the manner of the French Baroque, and even where the name of the dance is not given, as in No. 2, it is easy to recognize the Gavotte. The score found by Wilder contained 20 pieces, plus the overture. Mozart said that six pieces were by other composers, and that he had added 12, which proves Wilder's findings; for the latter eliminated the first six pieces as "miserable French arias," recognizing 13 pieces as genuine Mozart. The other pieces, such as No. 2, the old hit tune, "Charmante Gabrielle," were eliminated. It has been frequently pointed out that the melodies of the Parisian ballets anticipate later melodies such as that of the flute in No. 3 which reminds us of the one in *Magic Flute*, or No. 5 which resembles the last movement of the Piano Quartet in E-flat (K.493).

Les petits riens represent an interesting detour in Mozart's development in the field of the French ballet, and here in France we see Mozart, intentionally or not, involved with the ideas of the *ancien regime*. It is significant for Mozart's life history that fate prevented him from writing a French opera à la Grétry or Monsigny. He settled for a substitute with the meaningful title, *"Les petits riens."*

ITALIAN BALLET

Late in August 1771, Mozart composed a "Serenata teatrale," entitled *Ascanio in Alba,* commissioned by Empress Maria Theresa for the wedding of Archduke Ferdinand with the Princess Maria Ricciarda Beatrice of Modena. It was performed in Milan, with the opera, *Ruggiero,* by J. A. Hasse. On October 19, Leopold wrote that he could not describe to what degree the serenade had eclipsed the opera, but it is hard to tell whether this wasn't just another of Leopold's customary exaggerations. At any rate, the ballet played an important part. The dances originated with the solo dancer and choreographer, Jean Favier, but according to Schenk, with Noverre. *Ascanio* is a semi-dramatic work written by Abbate Giuseppe Parini. It is completely Byzantine, in the sense of the Italian and French Baroque. Just as in the era of Lully and Racine, Louis XIV provoked admiration on stage as Jupiter, here the Archduke himself, was Ascanio, a grandson of the goddess Venus; and Princess from Modena was the shepherdess Sylvia, from the House of the Alcides.

The ballet score consisted of eight numbers, but according to Abert, only the bass part, written by a copyist, has been preserved. As already mentioned, the musical director sometimes conducted from the Continuo-part, and sometimes from the violin part. Frequently these ballets were not written by the composer of the opera, which caused Leopold to emphasize in his letter of September 7 that "Wolfgang must compose the ballet that connects the two acts." Within the opera itself, there is a "Coro di Geni e Grazie Cantano e Ballano," a jubilant chorus in the manner of a Chaconne. Choruses are of predominant importance in this opera.

Ever since the days of the *camerata*, since the time of Monteverdi and of the Venetian opera, it had been customary to perform ballets during intermission. It was difficult to follow the involved plots and endless intrigues of the main work, and the intermezzi, whether they were ballets or comic scenes resembling the *comedia dell'arte*, offered a pleasant change of pace. At the Baroque courts, such ballets were regularly performed by the members of the ruling houses, and we know that Louis XIV was very proud of being the best dancer on stage. At the Austrian Court, the intermission ballet was of great importance. Since the days of Bertali, Cesti and Draghi opera performances were unthinkable without a ballet. Some letters of Leopold I to his Spanish ambassador, Pötting, describe such ballet performances. The libretti regularly list the names of the archdukes and aristocrats taking part. Usually, the choreography was planned by the Court choreographer, but the "invention" might originate with some nobleman.

In December, 1772, when Mozart performed his opera, *Lucio Silla* in Milan, he ran into all sorts of difficulties. The opera had been commissioned for the Milan winter season of 1772, and the libretto, by Gamerra, with adaptations by Metastasio, was dedicated to Archduke Ferdinand and his wife, the Princess of Modena. The Archduke was busy with his correspondence and kept the audience waiting for two and a half hours until he condescended to appear, and singers and orchestra were understandably very nervous. Then, the performers proved so incompetent that they created hilarity in the audience. In spite of this, the opera was a success, to which the ballet doubtlessly contributed its share although, as usual, it had no connection with the plot of the opera. The first ballet, directed by Carlo le Pic was called *Le Gelosie del Seraglio*. After the second act came a performance of a ballet by Giuseppe Salomoni, entitled *La Scuola di Negromanzia*, and the last ballet, again directed by Pic, named *La Giaconna*, allows us to assume that the opera closed with the customary chaconne. We know the contents of the ballet *Seraglio* from Noverre's famous *Lettres sur la Dance,* of 1760. In his new edition of Mozart's letters, Müller von Asow published for the first time the parts that have been preserved after the autograph at the Mozarteum in Salzburg. Mozart tried here what he succeeded in doing ten years later: to create Turkish local color with the means of 18th century music. It is noteworthy that the 8th section, which is obviously *alla turca,* was used in the last movement of the A Major Violin Concerto, and the key is A-flat, like the finale of the finale of the ballet. "Turkisms" reappear throughout Mozart's musical career. He introduced the Turk in *Seraglio* as well as in *Zaide.* Zaide and Zaire appear in the ballet in a manner corresponding to the famous drama *Zaire* by Voltaire. It is hard to imagine how the first piece, called *Reumatismo,* could have been performed as a dance. However, in the Italian letters of those days, we read Leopold's repeated complaints about his rheumatism. The names of the performers are listed exactly: the dancers and ballerinas Casacci, Salomoni, Morelli, Pic, Binetti and Moretto. Some of these dancers, like Pic and the famous Binetti also played a part in Casanova's life. Perhaps it might be worthwhile to reconstruct the ballet and to perform it according to Noverre's directions, even though Mozart's authorship has not been established beyond doubts. Neither Leopold nor Wolfgang mention the ballet in any of their letters, and as the ballets often were not written by the composer of the opera but by a second-rate musician, it is possible that the ballet is not Mozart's at all and that the corresponding section in Mozart's Concerto in A was borrowed from someone else's work. But the loan has been repaid with high interest.

Noverre's own description will help us to visualize the ballet: "The stage represents part of the Seraglio, a peristyle with cascades in the foreground. In the background a round colonnade. The space in between is decorated with garlands, flowers and fountains. In the rear, an expanse of water merges into a pool and a landscape forms the background. The women of the seraglio are seated on opulent sofas and cushions; doing needle-work, as customary in Turkey. White and colored eunuchs, beautifully garbed, appear and offer the sultan ice cream and coffee; harem girls bring flowers, fruit and perfume. One of them pays attention to no one but herself, refuses everything, and asks for a mirror; a slave hands her one. She looks at her-self with pleasure, studying her gestures and poses. Her com-panions, jealous of her gracefulness, imitate her; this is the basis for several scenes portraying voluptuousness and the girls' ardent desire to please their overlord.

The dainty music and the sounds of the water are followed by the proud melody of the silent eunuchs who announce the arrival of the great master. He enters hastily, followed by the Aga, a crowd of Janizaries, gnomes and four dwarfs. The dwarfs go down on their knees; the women bow and the dwarfs offer them flowers and fruit from their baskets. The pasha chooses a bouquet and with one gesture orders all the slaves to disappear. Alone, surrounded by his wives, he seems to hesitate which one to choose. They all try to conquer his heart, but he seems to prefer Zaide and Zaire. He hands the bouquet to Zaide, but at the moment she accepts it a glance from Zaire distracts him; he looks at her, and his eyes begin to wander again; he walks over to Zaide but a smile from Zaire makes him change his mind. He gives her the bouquet, and she takes it with delight. The poses of the other wives reveal anger and jealousy. Zaire gloats over their confusion and the defeat of her rival. The sultan, who had noticed the affect of his choice, wants to make Zaire's triumph complete and orders Fatima, Zima and Zaida to pin the flowers on the dress of his favorite wife. They obey sadly and despite their zeal to follow their master's order, their gestures show the defiance and despair which they try to suppress when their eyes meet his glance. The sultan dances a voluptuous pas de deux with Zaire and retires with her.

Zaide, whom the master almost gave the bouquet, dances a solo expressing bewilderment and angry defiance. She produces a dagger and tries to stab herself, but her companions grab her arm and hasten to dissuade her from committing suicide.

Zaide is ready to yield when Zaire proudly reappears; her presence rekindles her rival's anger. She lunges at her and tries to stab her as before she had wanted to stab herself. Zaire escapes with dexterity, grabs the dagger herself and raises her arms to stab Zaide. The women of the seraglio split into two groups, helping each. Zaide, disarmed, uses the moment when her rival's arm is being held and tries to get hold of the dagger in Zaire's hand to use it against her; but the other women foil her attempt. At this point, the eunuchs enter, attracted by the noise; they see the women fighting and, afraid of not being able to restore peace, they hurry out to call the sultan. The wives separate the two rivals who try to free themselves. They succeed. But once free, the two lunge at each other again. The frightened women try to prevent another fight. At this moment, the sultan arrives. The situation caused by his appearance is an amazing "coup de theatre." Wrath is instantly followed by happiness and tenderness. Zaire generously casts a friendly glance at her rival, which allays the sultan's fears of losing her. This peacefulness brings joy to the seraglio and the master permits the eunuchs to help prepare festivities to honor Zaire. Everybody joins in the dance.

In a *pas de deux*, Zaire and Zaide are reconciled. The master dances a *pas de trois* with them, definitely favoring Zaire.

The festival ends with an elegant contredance. The last figure displays a group standing on a high throne. It consists of women of the seraglio and the sultan; Zaire and Zaide are seated by his side. Slaves hold a canopy over the group. The sides of the stage are filled with another group of gnomes, white and colored eunuchs, mutes, janizaries, and midgets, all stretched out at the foot of the throne.

Mozart's most important ballet music is the one for *Idomeneo*. Dances in the old style suited the Baroque settings better than the Parisian ballets. In this opera, Mozart seems to have been fascinated by Gluck; the beginning of the introductory Chaconne is almost identical with Gluck's Chaconne for *Iphigenie en Aulide*. Since Lully's day, the Chaconne has been used as a final dance, but this adaptable form gave the choreographer hundreds of possibilities for interpretation. Mozart apparently tried to concentrate the heroic atmosphere of *Idomeneo* in the music of his Chaconne.

The Chaconne is followed by a small larghetto, thinner in instrumentation, its melody related to the South German folksong from the Ostrach manuscript, *Freu dich mein Herz, denk an kein Schmerz* (Be glad, my heart; don't think of grief) that appears in similar form as a theme with variations in Mozart's Piano Sonata in A. The Chaconne reappears; a *pas seul* follows; then a Passepied; a charming Gavotte later used as a *leitmotif* in Reinhardt's *Grüne Flöte* (Green Flute); and finally a Passacaglia. In the introductory Chaconne, we still find the parallel use of choreography and orchestration which is characteristic for the Baroque ballet. Whenever the complete ballet ensemble comes on stage, the full orchestra is playing; when a solo dancer appears we hear, as a rule, a trio of wind instruments; and when the oboe plays a staccato, we can imagine Mme. Falgera, the solo ballerina, dancing on her toes. The storm of the irate god of the ocean is described in a *pas seul de Mr. le Grand*, and the rolling figures and the threatening passages in unison let us anticipate terrifying events.

As an opera composer Mozart often had the occasion to write dance music. Who wouldn't remember the famous Fandango in the *Marriage of Figaro*? It is danced by Spanish country people who pay homage to Count Almavia. This Fandango was an original Andulsian melody that had been known in Vienna for a long time. This Spanish national dance and its variants—the Malagueña, Rondena, Granadina and Murciana --were brought to Europe during the 17th century and Spanish historians believe that it, as well as the Sarabande and the Chaconne, originated in South America or the West Indies. It is a sensual, alluring courting dance in ⅜ time, in which two bars are merged into one $^6/_8$ bar in the rhythm of the castinets. With the stanzas that are being danced and played alternate those that are being sung without dancing. The Fandango is a dance for two; its seductive and sensual insinuations mirror the ardent courtship of the man and the cunning restraint of the woman. Like the Sarabande, it came in for severe criticism. An amazing story is used by St. Leon, in 1858, in his ballet, *Le Procès du Fandango*. There are a Castilian and an Andulsian Fandango. The dancers of each sex have their separate turns and barely touch each other's hands. In Spain the Fandango fascinated young and old, and even swept persons of rank and dignity off their feet. In 1768, when Casanova was in Madrid, he attended a masked ball where the Fandango was danced: "I had thought I knew it but it turned out that I didn't know the first thing about it. I had only seen it on the stage in Italy and France, but the dancers were careful to avoid the gestures that make the Fandango the most seductive and the most sensual dance in the world. . ." If Casanova mentioned that he saw the Fandango only on stage, we may assume that he was referring to Gluck-Angiolini's *Don Juan*. The melody used by Mozart already appeared in this pantomine that was first performed in October 1761 at the Kärntnerthor-Theater. With this ballet, Angiolini followed the footsteps of Noverre and created a dramatic ballet that doubtlessly impressed Mozart deeply. Even the melody of the menuetto from *Don Giovanni* seems anticipated in a similar dance in Gluck's ballet, and Gluck's fandango was apparently simply taken over by Mozart. But how Mozart changed it! He stripped the dance of all the stereotyped rattle of castanets; and gave individual expression to low and middle voices, so that they convey a special feeling of motion. The wind instruments are treated with opulence. They either join in the dance, or separate from the rest and come in like a sigh indicating the old play of love. All this is written in a highly refined manner and points distinctly to the difference between the studied simplicity of Gluck and the high art of Mozart. As Marius Schneider explained in his article on the

Fandango in Blume's *Musik in Geschichte und Gegenwart* this dance was originally a *danza cantada* in ¾ or ⅜ time. The *Diccionario de Autoridades,* of the 18th century, names it as a South American import. The *Fandango de faena* is sung at work to make the horse go in a circle. When danced by a group, one of the participants may suddenly interrupt the fandango with the cry *bomba,* to direct a *copla* at his partner, after which the dance goes on. According to Schneider, the fandango appears in art music only as a dance for instruments. Rimsky-Korsakoff, in his *Capriccio Espagnol,* used an allegedly Asturian theme for a Fandango, and similar dances were used by Adam, Albéniz, Granados, DeFalla and E. Halfter. According to Schneider, the Fandango of Gluck and Mozart could be related to an 18th century manuscript at the Central Library in Barcelona. It goes as follows:

I conclude with Casanova's description of the dance:

"At the public balls in Madrid, very fashionable just now through new order by the police, each dancer has to bring his partner." Casanova did not have much trouble finding one; he describes the dance with his usual enthusiasm: "Around midnight, a charming spectacle unfolded before my eyes when the couples lined up accompanied by music and clapping of hands, to begin the maddest dance one can imagine."

"The dance cannot be described. Each couple, man and woman, takes just three steps and rattles with their castanets to the sound of the music; at the same time they strike a thousand different poses and go through movements of incredible sensuality! The first sighs of desire to the ecstasy of enjoyment. . . . The masked gentleman, who had taken me to the box, said to me: 'if you want to see the real fandango you should see it when it is danced by Gitanas (gypsies) and with partners who dance the same way.' " Whoever saw the Spaniards dance will agree with Casanova's description about the fire of Spanish dancing. Casanova was so delighted with it that in only three days he learned the fandango from a dancer of the opera, to such perfection that "according to the judgment of Spaniards, nobody can boast to do it better. . . ." When he demonstrated his new accomplishments at a ball a few days later, everybody was surprised to see a foreigner do the Spanish dance so well. The Spaniard always put more sentiment into dancing than anybody else. To them, social dancing is for exhibition and they do not try to conceal their half-oriental nature. Hence the importance attributed to gestures and especially to glances, by Spanish scholars of the dance such as Don Preciso in his *Elementos de la Ciencia Contredanzaria*.

Many treatises have been written about the theory and the origin of the fandango. Some trace it to the African "Chica"; others maintain that it had been imported to Spain as late as the 17th century from the *Reños de las Indias*;" that is, from America to Europe, like the Sarabande and the Folia—a perfectly plausible theory!

SOCIAL DANCE: THE MINUET

Out of three dances popular in Mozart's time, namely the
Minuet, the Contredance and the German dance, the Minuet
may be regarded as a monument of a previous era, while the
latter two were in popular use. The German was a favorite
dance with the middle and lower classes, as well as with the
young aristocrats. The Contre, already slightly obsolete, had not
entirely lost its popularity. The Minuet was considered old-
fashioned even then. Mozart superbly showed the social impli-
cations of the three dances in the ballroom scene of *Don
Giovanni* when the noble guests, Don Ottavio and Donna
Anna, dance the stately minuet to the sound of the full orchestra, slowly as was the custom among gentlefolk, Don Giovanni,
with Zerlina, dances the petty-bourgeois Contredance imported
from England, with all its democratic tendencies. The seducer
knows well that this gesture toward the bourgeoisie might win
for him the heart of the rustic beauty. The Contredance is
danced in $^2/_4$ time. In *Don Giovanni* it is accompanied by a
separate small orchestra, but simultaneously the third "couple,"
Masetto and Leporello, dance a typical Valse in $^3/_4$ time to a
primitive tune from the suburbs of Vienna or Prague. The two
small "orchestras" have only violins and bass, in contrast to the
instrumentation of the highly stylized minuet. Thus, those
three dances symbolize the three social classes of the budding
era of the Revolution: the minuet, the old ruling classes, the
contre the middle classes and the German dance, the third class
just rising. This scene has always been considered one of the
most charming scenes in *Don Giovanni*. The suburban mu-
sicans start by tuning their instruments, trying fifths, a piz-

zicato, a trill. The themes of the "German" are based on popular Viennese music, but the melody of the "Contre" can be found in many variations in contemporary books on the dance. It is marvelous how the different rhythms of the three dances are welded into a unified whole; every conductor knows the pitfalls of this passage.

The Minuet, which Mozart often danced himself, originated in the 17th century. Gottfried Taubert, the "honest dancing master" from Leipzig wrote in 1717 that it was one of the basic dances of the time, the others being the courante and the bourree. Taubert calls the minuet a daughter of the courante, but the relationship of the various dance forms are too entangled to be dealt with at this point.

We know for a fact, however, that hundreds of dancing masters danced the minuet in as many different ways, that their pamphlets described their new steps and positions with pride and utmost accuracy and that since the Basse Dance of the Middle Ages no dance had been as vastly intellectualized as the minuet.

Taubert alone dedicated 150 pages to the different figures of this dance. We can imagine that the more dynamic new generation which had been brought up in the time of rationalism, and began to yearn for freedom and the enjoyment of life, considered the minuet as obsolete as pigtail and wigs. The fact that the Minuet, the most popular dance of its time, escaped oblivion in a new era is highly significant for the history of music. It was the only dance that saved itself from the continuity of the suite via the divertimento and the serenade, into the modern sonata and symphony, and finally the modern scherzo. Thus, in Mozart's time the minuet had a two-fold function: as an occasional, highly stylized social dance, and as part of a movement in a sonata, symphony, divertimento or serenade.

The Minuet is believed to have been a popular dance originating in Poitou, perhaps connected with the *Branle de Poitou* which also was in triple time. According to Arbeau, the branle must be danced with wooden shoes. The name Minuet means "small step." As Sachs says in his *World History of the Dance*: "The minuet is unsurpassed in combining dignity with grace, subdued levity with respectful gallantry; and it may be the most beautiful expression of the *style simple* which was introduced by Louis XIV."

The Minuet was danced by pairs, and open. Solemn greetings of spectators and partner, dainty steps to the left and to the right, sliding steps forwards and backwards, holding hands—a repetition of the age-old game of flirtation, of giving or denying oneself. In the last analysis it is a highly stylized expression of the relationship of the sexes in the overly-refined manner of Baroque society. The standard work in Mozart's time was the "Allerneueste Anweisung zur Aeusserlichen Moral," by Gottlieb Hänsel. Hänsel was dancing master at the Leipzig University and his widely-read book appeared in Leipzig in 1755. "That the minuet consists of four steps," he wrote, "two flexible and two rigid ones, is known even to those whom we are wont to call *gate-metiers*, or bunglers. But which foot comes first and how to teach the rest of the delicate and appealing positions, makes the difference between a real connoisseur and such a bungler. In certain public houses around Leipzig, one sometimes meets such gentlemen who do not care whether their pupils dance these two flexible and rigid steps or learn to limp or hop. They don't know how to explain it and consider it sufficient to count one, two, three, four. Trash! Where will such audacity lead?" We learn from Hänsel's famous book that the minuet was the focal dance of the time and that dancing instruction started with it as it had started two generations before with the courante or sarabande. As early as 1728, the Neapolitan dancing master, Giambattista Dufort, in his *Trattato del Ballo Nobile*, had called the minuet the "entrance door" of dancing instruction. Hänsel lists different steps of the minuet used in social dancing, as well as in the theater; VI, 2: "*Plié*, bending the knees; *glissé*, a sliding step, executed by sliding the foot along the floor; *elevé*, an elevation achieved by stretching the

88

knees; *tombé*, a "fallen step," when the body has lost its balance and has to fall because of its own weight." To quote other dancing masters of the time would go too far. It may be more important to point out tempo and rhythm of the minuet. In his, "Versuch einer Anweisung die Flöte traversière zu spielen" (1752), Quantz says: "A minuet should be played fast and each quarter stressed by somewhat heavy, short bowing; there should be one pulse beat to two quarters." This being based on a pulse beat of 80, we get MM = 160, a tempo confirmed by Hänsel in 1755, when he says of the Polonaise that "it is played only half as fast as the Minuet, since I finish two bars of the Minuet in the time one bar of the Polish dance would take." Kuhnau, in his *Neue Klavierübung* also calls the tempo of the minuet somewhat quick (1689). Dancing masters like C. F. Forster (Der Tanzlehrer, Breslau, 1828) state that the tempo of the Minuet slowed down near the end of the 18th and during the 19th century.

The long career of the Minuet started with the suite, even though its youth prevented it from gaining a leading position equalling that of its big four constituents (Allemande, Courante, Sarabande, Gigue). But it won the most important place among the intermezzi which were interpolated ad libitum between Sarabande and Gigue. The importance of the minuet is proved by the fact that several Minuets were frequently presented *en suite* within a cyclic form such as the suite or serenade. Even most of Haydn's first quartets have two minuets. But, along with cultural developments, the melodic structure of the Minuet undergoes basic changes. In France, the power and the greatness, the solemnity and pathos of Lully's melodic expression changes into daintiness, gracefulness, playfulness. This is the transition from the Baroque to Rococo. Just as the Minuet was originally danced on the figure 8, later on an S, then on a 2, and—after a reform by the dancing master Pécour (around 1700)—on a Z, its melody also changed. I shall compare three minuets; one by Lully, one by Campra, one by Rameau.

In contrast to Lully's melodic development, which is typically Baroque, Campra's dance is built on various small sections. Groups are organized symmetrically, the polyphonic structure is loosened and the contrapuntal motion replaced by chordal patterns. Campra's Rococo prevails throughout the time of Rameau. Rhythm submerges under accents dissolved into melody. Let's compare those French dances with the Minuets of Haydn's immediate predecessors and compatriots. The difference is most apparent when we compare the minuet from Rameau's Castor and Pollux (1737) with one by Mathias Monn (1740).

Rameau's Minuet leads the melody in delicate turns beyond the first bar and we can visualize the courteous gestures of the dancing couple, and even their glances (Eros restrained by the culture of a refined society). Actually, Monn's sharply accented, stamped rhythms, his broad melody with its big intervals originating from the yodle, stem from the masculine culture of al-

90

pine population. What does Rameau's Minuet still have in common with Monn's except the name? Here we see the new spirit of the century forced into the rigid mold of the Minuet. It does not matter whether the Minuets of Monn, Starzer, Wagenseil or the young Haydn were derived from the alpine *Stampfer* or whether some of them go back to the Czech *Rejdovák*. Such Czech dances appear in some manuscripts of the 17th century, such as those *Bransles da Polion* (1658) by the conductor of the Palace Cathedral in Prague. (See Paul Nettl: *Musikbarock in Böhmen und Mähren*, p. 23) . Their origin and nationality are of lesser importance than their cultural and social setting.

At any rate, Mozart's Minuets are founded on Alpine dance habits. This applies to the Minuets for actual use as well as to those in the symphonies; such as, named at random, the Haffner Symphony (K.385) and the Symphony in E-flat Major (K.543) .

THE CONTRE DANCE AND THE GERMAN DANCE

In Chapter XII of his *Answeisung* (Instructions), Hänsel wrote: "The English dances are generally called the English *Sesjen* or Contre Dances; at Court balls and weddings they are danced more frequently than any others except the minuet. They are two variants: the single and the double."

Actually, the English Contre Dance originally was a country dance either a "round" or a "longway." Those two forms of the round dance are mentioned in John Playford's textbook for dancing, *The English Dancing-Master or Directions for Country Dances* (1651). In the "round" (branle), the pairs go in circles; in the "longway" men and women face each other in a straight line. Both forms consist of various figures: groups of three, changing position, circling around, etc. Those figures were inexhaustible, and every dancing master tried to invent new ones.

Already in the 17th century those Contre Dances were called "Anglaises." What is the English element in them? Round dances existed at all times and with all peoples. The African Negro and the Spaniard knew them equally well, and the Czech folk dances included so-called "chain rounds," such as the Chitava, the Moták and the Motovidlo. Their focus is the old game of flirtation, of rejecting and finding one another—advancing, evading, separating, joining. In the Bohemian Chitava the men and women pursue each other. Wedding dances of the 17th century include "chain" chances with the oddest figures. On the stage rounds are danced; groups of soloists detach themselves as in the tragedy of the antique. The final Chaconnes in the operas from Lully's time to Mozart's *Ido-*

meneo are such rounds. Why did the English rounds become so popular in 18th century Europe? Sachs believes that one feature which appeared nowhere else was typically English: the gradual emergence of the pairs, the intriguing combination of ensemble dancing and that of individual couples. He qualified this statement by explaining that dancing pairs who detach themselves from the rank and file also appear in the Rhodesian Baila, but in Europe, this principle was limited to England; Spanish sources of about 1600 called this dance form branle "de Inglaterra."

The characteristic feature is the unlimited number of dancers that can participate. The simultaneous execution of certain figures requires a certain number; a round dance, at which as many people as possible should participate, requires patient waiting in line—a democratic principle which the West takes for granted. This English manner probably has always been considered democratic; already at the Court of Queen Elizabeth masters and servants danced together. In 1726, Dufort described the Contre Dance alongside the Minuet—but as a professional dancing master he was bound to be prejudiced against the latter with its lack of *coupés, balancés, tiptoe* steps; it consisted of simple walking, the essential feature being the expressive coordination of the pairs and their integration into the ensemble. Fundamentally this dance contains the principle of the new social order. People had become tired of the choreographic arrangements that moved with minute, almost mathematical, precision, just as they had tired of the trigonometrical alignments of their cities and gardens. The old baroque dances were danced by individual pairs; in the old "hostelries" and "kingdoms" the prince first danced with his lady, while everybody else looked on. "L'Etat c'est moi," also meant, "the dance is mine." The old dance was painstakingly regulated and when a Court masquerade was held, the guests were told in detail how to dress and which dance to perform with which partner. The Contre Dance changed all this. Whoever had straight limbs and common sense was admitted.

93

But the English dance shared the fate of all the other dances of the 17th and 18th centuries. Not until it reached Paris was it admitted to society. This was expressed even in the name: in Paris, the rural "country dance" became a "contre-dance" with emphasis on the *contre*—dancing "against" each other; and gradually this interpretation was adopted in England, while its meaning as a country dance got lost. Under the influence of the contre-dance, the old English "round" was resuscitated early in the 18th century and called the "Round for Eight;" but in Paris it was danced so differently that it was called "Contre-dance Française" and received the French name *Cotillon* (petticoat), allegedly after the song:

La Commère, quand je danse
Mon Cotillon va-t-il bien?

Godmother, when I dance
how does my petticoat look?

In the Cotillion two groups, of four pairs each, take crosswise positions, greet each other on the first *entree*, execute their refrain to the second part of the music, and return to their old places (Sachs). The Cotillion had an enormous number of tours and often ended in a game of forfeits whose various phases—as Robitschek explained in his psychoanalytical study of the Cotillion—belong in the field of hidden sexuality. Could this, perhaps, explain the name of the dance?

According to Hänsel, the Cotillion consists mostly of a *Menuet en quatre ou en huit;* figures in different combinations.

"As far as their steps are concerned, these are all French; for example they contain *Pallones* (balls), *Bourée-Pas, Chasses,* double and single; *Pas de fleuret, Jettes, Pas de Rigaudon, Pirouettes;* partly also totally new steps which mostly derive from the old ones however, and were created at the German dancing masters' discretion." In his *Anstandslehre,* Hänsel asks his esteemed patrons to do him the honor of paying him a visit so he could explain and describe the Cotillion. Finally, toward the end of the 19th century, the old Cotillion developed into a series of dances as symmetrical as the old suite: This was the Quadrille, so named because the couples, dancing in columns, form small quadrangles at four dancers (2 pairs) each. The Quadrille is still danced today. Originally it consisted of five parts, but around 1800, dancing master Trénitz added a sixth. The present form of the Quadrille consists of the following parts:

The Pantalon, so called after the couplet

Le pantalon
de Toinon
N'a pas de fond

The trousers
of Toinon
Have no bottom.

the Eté, the Poule, the Pastourelle (in 32 bars in $^6/_8$ or $^2/_4$ measure, rural in character), and finally the Trénitz. People do not dance during the first eight bars of each part. The music was often a potpourri of melodies from popular concert pieces, operettas or operas.

The quadrille and the contre, from which it derived, had one thing in common: freedom from a definite melodic or rhythmic scheme. Actually, its principle is similar to that of the basse-dances of the 16th century in which an existing melody was transformed according to the dancing master's wishes. Like the old Jig, the old English country dance had two or three beats. Already Georg Muffat published a Contre in his *Florilegium Secundum* (1698), and called it, characteristically, a *saltus a giga non absimilis*. In Mozart's time, the "German" was as popular as the Minuet and the Contre. The biographer of Leopold I, Rinck, states that the Emperor who occasionally attended dance entertainments, preferred a sort of "German direction." What was the nature of the dances at the Hapsburg Court? About 1608, they had masquerades at which people danced in the Italian fashion. In a letter to her brother Ferdinand, Archduchess Maria Magdalena, staying in Graz, wrote that dances played a great role in entertainment, as did comedies and sleighrides, and that she intended to remember the two *Intrate* danced there until his arrival.

"One is crazy ("narisch"), the other charming; I know you will like both. The Englishmen came to two of our maquerades and asked to see me and the other woman dance in the Italian manner. After four of us had danced it four times, without the Intrata and faster than the Spanish, Ambrosy and I alone danced the wonderful dance he invented for me. Then Trautl and I danced a galiarde together; then came a tortilion for four. We danced these dances because we wanted to be the Italian peasant girls whose garb we wear, as you will see. In the beautiful masquerade, we danced the Intrata, six persons carrying torches; it must have been wonderful to look at. Then Ambrosy and I danced Canary, then six of us danced the *waleta in sory* (illegible in old ms.). Our brother Max and Ambrosy danced with us. Then again, six of us danced the *galleria di amor*, then four of us (Max, Ambrosy and Countess Portia) danced the *florido lilio*, and finally the *fiama di amor*, also with torches. You can't imagine how fascinated the Englishman was with our dancing; however, we didn't do the Italian dances one after another, but danced some German in between."

This makes it clear that German dances were performed alongside the Italian pantomimes which featured the *Canario, Gagliarda, Tortiglione,* as well as torch dances. A little later, the Court performed "peasants weddings," hostelries, "Kingdoms," "Landschaften," "pastorals." Even though the festivities of the Austrian Baroque had their roots in the culture of the Courts, they reveal strongly popular features. Name and meaning of "pastorals" are self-evident. For the "Peasants Weddings" bride and groom, the parents of the bride, bridesmaid and best man were chosen by the Court Chamberlain and all the other participants were guests at the wedding. For the "Kingdom" a royal couple was chosen and the "Court employees" were determined by lot. The favorite entertainment was the "hostelry," which a Jesuit, Claude François Ménestrier, who saw one in 1670 in Munich, called "the most agreeable and spirited manner of the world." (*Des representations en Musique Anciennes et Modernes*, Paris, 1681.) In those festivities, the Imperial couple were the hosts and the Court Chamberlain determined what the guests had to wear. There were Spaniards, Dutch, Hungarians, Italians, even Americans—and they all wore the fancy costumes which we know from Burnacini's *Maschere*. The most famous masquerade of the 17th century probably was the "Hostelry" staged in 1698 for Czar Peter the Great. The Imperial couple, clad as tavernists, greeted the "Ruler over all Russians" in the main hall of the *Hofburg* which had been converted into a garden. The Czar's partner was Miss von Thurn. The dance was followed by a banquet at which Czech pages served the Czar since no Russian-speaking titled interpreter could be found. Merian, in Frankfurt, has illustrated the scene in an engraving which shows the banquet at left, the dance hall at right. It does not show the dance band, but the poses of the pairs indicate that the dance was bucolic in character.

How did the people dance on such occasions? The numerous manuscripts of the mid-17th century prove that the dances were not written by the great Italian opera composers, such as Bertali, Ziani, Cesti, Draghi, Caldara, but by native Viennese. They wrote the dances not only for the hostelries, pastorals and masquerades but also for the ballets and pantomimes for the entr'acts of the operas. The list of those composers included Wolfgang Ebner (1610-1655), Johann Heinrich Schmelzer (1623-1680) and his son Andreas Anton Schmelzer (1653-1701), Johann Joseph Hoffer, and the Anglo-Italian violinist and ballet composer, Nikolaus Matteis. Among them, the older Schmelzer was the most prominent. Many different dances were en vogue. From France came the Minuet (though not in classical Versailles style), as well as the *Gavotte*, the *Allemande*, the *Rigaudon*, the *Passepied*, and the *Bourrée*. From Italy came the *Gagliarda*, the *Pavana*, the *Saltarello*; from Spain, the

Chaconne, the *Sarabande*, the *Folia*; and from England the *Gigue*.

Without elaborating on the story of the dancing masters at the Vienna Court, we might mention that Santo Venturo, who was born in Venice in 1626, came to Vienna under Ferdinand II and was active under Leopold I. The records mention a new style on floor and stages, which he introduced around 1652. Santo was a pupil of Carlo Beccaria who, in turn had studied with Cesare Negri, the famous "Trombone" whose *Nuove Invenzioni di balli* (1604) and *Grazie d'amore* (1602) are the classic dance textbooks from the Renaissance.

In 1678, Santo Ventura was succeeded by his son, Domenico Ventura. Even though the dignified manner of the Italian school prevailed at the Austrian Court, the lighter French style had not remained unknown. In the correspondence between Leopold I and his Spanish Ambassador, Poetting, there is amusing evidence of the envy and jealousy in certain Court circles against the French ballet. For instance, in September 1666, the French Ambassador, Grenonville, gave a French ballet, and the Spanish Ambassador resented that the Emperor attended the performance.

But what were the "German directions" like, which the biographer of Leopold I, mentioned? Undoubtedly there must have been some connection between Court and folk dances. The Austrian and South German folk dance seems to have been identical with the old *Weller*, which had come to the cities from Bavaria and from the mountains and valleys of Styria Province. The illustrations by H. S. Beheim give us an idea of those dances. Montaigne also saw such a dance, in 1580, at the Palais Fugger in Augsburg (*Journal de voyage de Michel Montaigne.*) The partners place their hands on each other's back, and come so close to each other that their faces touch. To the present day, Austrian peasants dance the *Ländler* in this manner. Mastersinger Kunz Has complained in 1525, "Now they dance the crazy *Weller*—the *Spinner*, as they call it." We may assume that the *Weller* was a gliding dance, like the waltz later. As it was taken over by Society, the wide steps and abrupt movements were modified and refined. The above-mentioned illustration of the "hostelry" in honor of Peter the Great actually shows several pairs who hold hands and move in large steps with very lively movement. It is likely that such a *Weller,* which had been accepted at Court, was danced to a melody in moderate two beats, with the gentleman first leading his lady around the hall, and starting to whirl her around temperamentally when the melody changed to quick triple time. The musical form of the rythmic-metric variations, which corresponds to the increasing excitement of the dancers, goes back to the old form of dance and after-dance. The wide inter-vals of the melody in many of Schmelzer's *Arie Viennesi* are such old German dances; on the one hand their music cor-responds to the wide dance steps; on the other hand, it closely resembles the melodic structure of the Alpine yodler. To illus-trate, here is a Schmelzer dance which I published in the *Denkmäler der Tonkunst in Oesterreich*:

Among the Viennese dance composers, only Johann Heinrich Schmelzer wrote such popular music. Neither his son nor Hoffer produced music with the slightest *Weller* characteristics.

Some traces, however, can be found in the music of the foreigner, Matteis, who interpolated the following Aria (*Ländler*) into Caldara's opera, Venceslaus (1717):

The *Weller* lasted until the reign of Charles VI, when the Austrian Court came under the influence of French culture, and the French choreographer, Phillibois, ruled over dance floor and ballet. *Weller* and *Ländler* came to be restricted to the Vienna suburbs and Austrian provinces. The *Ländler* was danced in ²/₈, ²/₄ or even in ³/₈ time and was characterized by stamping. The *Weller* was a gliding dance in ³/₈ or ³/₄. The word, "*Ländler*" comes from *Landl* (small country), meaning the provinces of Upper Austria and neighboring Styria. The word "waltz" does not appear in the 17th century—not until the middle of the 18th. Manuscripts of folk dances often show the name of *Arie Styriache*. In colloquial German, waltzing is synonymous with strolling, but also with gliding, in contradistinction to stepping or jumping.

Around 1780, waltzing was still considered most objectionable, as proven by edicts by the bishops of Würzburg and Fulda. But already five years later, the young Goethe, then a student in Strassburg, felt that he must be able to dance the waltz to make a better impression in society. In his *Werther*, he described how the protagonist and Lotte were dancing together and how "the spheres whirl around each other." Since neither of them danced well, they decided to dance a waltz to a "German"; from then on everything went well and the pair enjoyed the variegated swinging motions. We must bear in mind, however, that in dancing the "German" the motions of hands and arms were of utmost importance. In describing the new *Allemande*, the dance chroniclers of those days did not concentrate on the steps, but on the gestures. The folded arms seem to indicate that the dances were originally accompanied by hand clapping; the crossing of arms could be a choreographic stylization of the clapping.

Strassburg actually seems to have been the door through which the German dances reached France: *Strasbourgeoise* and *Alsacienne* were the favorite dances in mid-18th century Paris.

In his *Essay sur la Musique* (1780), La Borde published such Strassburg dances in both two and three beats. In a letter, dated October 19, 1777, Mozart mentioned a Strassburg concerto, which undoubtedly is the violin concerto K. 218. The Rondeau has a musette theme which is very similar to a musette called *Ballo Strasburghese*, in Dittersdorf's *Carnival Symphony*. Incidentally, Dittersdorf seems to have had a predilection for this theme, since he also used it in the Rondo of his Symphony in D Major, which was republished in the Austrian *Denkmäler*. An Almanac for the year 1682 shows the existence of Strassburg minuets with a bucolic character, which makes them quite different from those of Lully and his contemporaries. Undoubtedly the Rhinelanders danced the minuet as sort of a *Ländler*.

Volk und Heimat (People and Country), a book published in honor of Viktor von Geramb, contains an interesting contribution about the Strasbourgeoise by Raimund Zoder, who referred to an 1813 chronicle from upper Styria (Knaffl manuscript). This chronicle compares the dances from Upper Styria and Strassbourg; in both genres, gestures and folding of arms are essential, which seems to characterize them as courtship dances. As early as 1794, F. D. Graeter wrote in his essay, *On the German Folk Songs and their Music* that a love affair seems to have been the motivation for this dance. The Strassbourgeoise doubtlessly came to Austria as a ballroom dance and, according to Caroline Pichler, was also used in Vienna between 1770 and 1780. "While several circles of people dancing the "German" formed in the spacious Redoutensaal, some very youthful couples tried the *Strassburger* in the center where they were not disturbed by the quick rotation of the waltzing pairs; it consisted merely of graceful crossing of arms and body postures. Only agile young people could do this with good results, for which reason it was not in general usage."

About the years 1807-9 she reported that the *Strassbourgeoise* and the *Menuette a la Reine* were no longer popular. In 1779, the Theater in der Josephstadt performed *The Ball*, a comedy in which "Herr Salomoni and Madle Neubauer dance a minuet and a *strassburgish*." (Bluemml-Gugitz: *Alt-Wiener Thespis Karren, Vienna*, 1925.) The *Strasbourgeoise* was mentioned frequently in those days, but disappeared around 1840. The Styrian survived; I found its oldest tune in the archives of Kremsier and published it in the Austrian *Denkmäler*. Mozart's remark about the Strassburg concerto indicates that the melody was very popular in Vienna just then; he frequently used folk tunes in the last movement of his violin concertos.

Goethe was well familiar with the waltz and later immortalized it in his *Hochzeitslied* (Wedding song):

"So rennet nun alles in vollem Galopp
Und kürt sich im Saale sein Plätzchen;
Zum Drehen und Walzen und lustigen Hopp
Erkieset sich jeder ein Schätzchen."

And so they all race in full gallop
and pick their place in the hall;
To whirl and to waltz and to gaily hop
Every boy looks for a gal.

His enthusiasm was by no means shared by all his contemporaries. Sir John Dean Paul, who had seen the dance on the Tivoli in 1802, wrote: "The dance we saw is more than strange. About 200 pairs were turning round to the accompaniment of very slow music. My drawing can give but a vague illustration of what really happened. The posture of the women was agreeable and graceful, but the less said of the men, the better. They were repulsive, dirty, and common."

Michael Kelly, Mozart's Irish friend and pupil, did not express himself more favorably on the subject. In his *Reminiscences* (London, 1826) he wrote as follows:

"The people of Vienna were in my time dancing-mad; as the Carnival approached, gaiety began to display itself on all sides, and when it really came, nothing could exceed its brilliancy. . . . The propensity of the Vienna ladies for dancing and going to carnival masquerades was so determined that nothing was permitted to interfere with their enjoyment of their favorite amusement—nay, so notorious was it, that, for the sake of ladies in the family way, who could not be persuaded to stay at home, there were apartments prepared, with every convenience for their accouchement, should they be unfortunately required. And I have been gravely told, and almost believe, that there have actually been instances of the utility of the arrangement. The ladies of Vienna are particularly celebrated for their grace and movements in waltzing, of which they never tire. For my own part, I thought waltzing from 10 at night until 7 in the morning, a continual whirligig; most tiresome to the eye and ear—to say nothing of any worse consequences."

I am quoting Kelly, because he was a cultured Englishman who happened to be in Vienna in Mozart's time. He had an enormous amount of admiration for the Austrian capital, but little taste for the charm of its favorite dance.

Now a few words about the early appearance of the word "waltz." We find it in Grétry's *Airs pour Danser* (1784), but this was not the first time the word was mentioned. In Kurz-Bernardon's comedy, *The Revived Bernardon* (1754), with music probably by Haydn, the word "waltz" was sung to a real waltz tune. Here are the words:

"Bald singen, bald springen,
Bald saufen, bald ranzen,
Bald spielen, bald tanzen,
Bald walzen umadum,
Mit heissa, Rum, Rum."

They sing, they jump
they drink, they travel,
they play, they dance,
they waltz around,
hey! huzza! rum, rum.

And here is the melody:

17th Century manuscripts clearly show the melody based on thirds, sixths, and octaves, which derive from the yodler or a wind instrument. The yodler, the characteristic musical expression of the mountaineers, was used not only by the population of the Alpine countries but also by those of the Apalachians. Curt Sachs and other musicologists have expressed the opinion that large intervals correspond to the wide, vehement gestures in the dances of people with masculine cultures. For this reason, the *Ländler* and the *Weller*—the ancestors of the German dance and the waltz—show vehement leaps and rolling movements. Broken triads and wide intervals characterize not only the classic waltz, such as Weber's *Invitation to a Dance*, many dances by Lanner and Johann Strauss, or the overture in *Ländler* rhythm to Bach's *Peasant Cantata* but also the majority of the symphonic minuets of Haydn, Mozart and Schubert. A close connection between this type of melody and the accent on the strong beat is characteristic of the German dance and the waltz. The rhythm of the baroque dance spreads over larger spaces; it does not have the rhythmic elan of the modern dances. The natural dancer, charged with energy, instinctively follows the laws of gravity and squeezes the overflow of his energies into the strong beat. Compare the terms of male and female ending. This development corresponds to the evolution of musical history of the 17th and 18th centuries, which turns from polyphony to homophony. For the up and down of dissonance and consonance corresponds to the up and down of the rhythmic accents. While the groups within the baroque dances are wide, and the bars merely serve orientation, the new dances, such as the German and the waltz, are rhythmically rigid; this phenomenon corresponds to the philosophy of the petty bourgeoisie with its predilection for limited entities—quite in contrast to the unlimited will, unlimited power, unlimited knowledge of the aristocratic culture of the Baroque.

For a long time, it was presumed that the first waltz ever danced on stage was the one in Martin's *Una cosa rara* (1786). But this writer established the fact that a genuine choral waltz appeared in 1660, in the fragment of a *singspiel* which is preserved in the State Library in Vienna (ms. 18964). It is a scene between a pair called Trautl and Hensl, part of a bucolic play in three acts, the first act of which is lost. The final chorus is a saucy waltz, first sung, then danced. Here, too, we find the typical triad melody with the accent on the first beat (Paul Nettl: *Zur Vorgeschichte der sueddeutschen Taenze, Bulletin de l'Union Musicologique*, vol. III, p. 45 ff.). There exists an obvious contrast between the old regulated dances which were used for the "hostelries" and "pastorals," the gavottes, minuets, and passepieds, with their precise instructions and fancy gestures; and the new German and waltzes which are based on genuine emotion. An old, rigid minuet compares to a German dance like a clavier to a modern pianoforte; like the "regulated human" who received his instructions from higher powers—religion, authorities, corporations, habits—the clavier player of the Baroque needed the various registers to transfer his energy to the instrument. Likewise, the dancer of the Baroque danced according to definite rules. The "classic human" formed his own world; he "seized fate by the throat," as Beethoven said; he dared the gods, like Goethe in *Prometheus*; likewise, the modern pianist transfers his energy directy to the instrument; his piano and forte need no relay station. In the realm of the dance, this new spiritual and physical approach found its expression in the dynamic German and above all, in the Waltz.

Since the 17th century—and probably much earlier, if we are to believe Johannes de Grocheo, a 14th century writer—dancers and dance composers did not stick to single dances but preferred groups and "chains." People danced *en suite*. Already Arbeau, the French Renaissance choreographer, mentioned dance suites in which the various *Branles* (folk dances) followed each other according to definite rules. "The musicians are used to start the dances with a double branle (usually called "common branle"); then comes a simple branle, then a gay branle, and finally the *Branle de Bourgogne* (Burgundy), which some people also call *Branle de Champagne*. The succession of those four types of branle corresponds to the age groups of the participants: the older people dance the stately double and simple branles; young married couples the gay branles, and the very young people the light-footed Burgundy; everybody dispatches his chore as well as he can, according to his age and agility."

In Germany, however, only the old dance and after-dance were known just as the German peasant and petty bourgeois only knew his casserole meal while the French and English gourmets preferred several courses. The same thing happened with dancing. The suite, which is more sophisticated, derived from French models of the 16th century, while the English dramatist, George Chapman (1559-1634) wrote in his *Alphonsus, Emperor of Germany*:

106

> 'We Germans have no changes in our dances,
> An almain and an up-spring that is all.' "

This refers to the old usage of having a dance in slow steps followed by a fast dance in leaps; the melody, originally in two beats, was converted into three fast beats. This principle of the variation suite, however, can be found in older dances, including French, English and Italian ones. The variation dance suite corresponds to the philosophy of dependency that prevailed during the Middle Ages and the Baroque period: a given theme runs through all the dances and the musician has no possibility of inventing new melodies. This principle has its counterpart in the old *cantus firmus* Mass, in which all the parts are based on a certain melody, either sacred or secular.

Even though the principle of the suite was based on the philosophy of the Baroque, its effects were felt into the era of classicism. For the chains of Minuets, the Contres, the German, are nothing but degenerated suites, the latter two corresponding to the new ideas of individual freedom. However, before going into details about the Mozart dances, let's examine the dance halls before and during his lifetime.

DANCE HALLS

One of the oldest sources on dancing and dance music in 18th century Vienna is Johann Basilius Küchelbecker's *Allerneueste Nachricht vom römisch-Kayserlichen Hofe. Nebst einer ausführlichen Historischen Beschreibung der Kayserlichen Residentz-Stadt Wien, und der umliegenden Örter.* (Newest report from the Roman Imperial Court, plus a detailed history of the Imperial capital of Vienna and surrounding places.) I am using the second edition, which was published in 1732 by Johann Jacob Foerster, of Hannover. Küchelbecker, a syndic of St. Annaberg, who lived in Vienna for a long time, first describes the Imperial "hostelries." Charles VI seems to have been a good dancer. "When a hostelry is given, their Imperial Majesties pose as inn-keepers, the other cavaliers and ladies are sent there and appear in disguise; every pair is told what to wear, and the gentleman has to give his lady her clothes as a present. Such occasions are always very gay, and His Majesty gives a good example to his guests who are supposed to dance and play throughout the evening. Admission to an Imperial hostelry is somewhat difficult—and the same is true of the show, played by young noblemen in the so-called 'small theatre' that is very limited in space. But it is not impossible to get in if you approach the Chamberlain or an Ambassador and walk in with him."

Küchelbecker goes on to describe dance entertainments arranged by ladies of the nobility in their private homes. Those private balls were still en vogue in Mozart's time; in the abovementioned letter to his father, dated January 22, 1783, he wrote about a ball in his apartment for which the *chapeaux* had to pay

2 gulden admission. Küchelbecker wrote: "During the winter season we have another pastime: private dances arranged by very special people to whom you have to pay one gulden for dancing and refreshments; and you can have a lot of fun for your money. One lady of the nobility and her husband actually make a living by giving several such balls, also during the summer; the most elegant cavaliers attend. But it must be emphasized that the entertainment is distinguished throughout, that nothing extraordinary happens, and that there is no reason for hesitating to spend a ducat on it once in a while."

Vienna's most popular dance hall was located on the Mehlgrube (flour pit). The building stood on the Neue Markt and was originally used as a municipal storehouse for flour. Rebuilt after blueprints by Fischer von Erlach in 1698, the large hall in the first floor was used for entertainment, especially at Carnival time; Kisch's *Die alten Strassen und Plätze Wiens* (The Old Streets and Squares of Vienna) contains much information on the subject. Küchelbecker's description follows: "During the Carnival several festivities happen which, however, are far less amusing than they are said to be. They mostly consist of balls, gatherings, dances, games, eating, drinking. Sometimes people wear masks, sometimes not—depending on His Majesty's permission, without which nobody is allowed to wear them. The most elegant ball takes place in the spectacular house which the municipality built on the Mehl-Grube; the host is the chamberlain of Prince Eugene, who collects one ducat. The high nobility of Vienna appears there; others are admitted but it is considered desirable that they would produce authentic genealogical proof of their sixteen ancestors when asking a lady for a dance; otherwise she may take too long to decide whether to dance with him, or refuse in order to avoid the mortal sin of permitting an obscure nobleman to touch her more high aristocratic hand. If people wear masks, those self-styled gods are slightly more gracious; but if an unmasked commoner would dare to dance with a lady of standing, he would have to run head over heels, having committed no less than a crime against the nobility. During the Carnival of 1728, it actually happened that an untitled gentleman who dared to dance with such a lady was shown the door."

Children also had their dance entertainments:

"In addition, a so-called Children's Festival is held on the Mehlgrube during the carnival. Parents who want to treat their children to an appropriate diversion, place an order for such entertainment with food, drink, and music with the same person who gives the other balls. Toward evening, a large number of elegant boys and girls with their usual chaperones appear, beautifully garbed, and amuse themselves with eating, drinking and dancing, until 9 or 10 p.m. at which time they return home. Many ladies and gentlemen meantime appear to enjoy the spectacle of this harmless children's festival; later those adult children start where the young ones left off and continue to dance and play games until the small hours."

Küchelbecker unfortunately did not describe the popular festivities which were held in the suburb of Brigittenau.

"Parish fairs and similar festivities are celebrated in Vienna and suburbs, such as St. Brigitta which is near Leopoldstadt on the Danube bank on a colorful meadow in the wood. The same goes for the hospital at St. Marcus. But this is only an entertainment for the common people of whom many thousands appear, so we won't dwell on it any longer. However, many aristocrats are so curious that they visit those places if a fair is held, and there you can see the most elegant ambassadors and many persons of rank who derive enjoyment from watching plebeian entertainment."

Vienna's reputation as a city of phaecians and the "Cupua of the intellect" does not derive from the Congress of Vienna and Grillparzer, but from Abraham a Santa Clara and old Wolfgang Schmeltzl who wrote in 1548, in the style of Hans Sachs:

> "Here are many singers and string players,
> Plenty of company, many pleasures . . ."

110

In his *Esquisse d'un tableau mouvant de Vienne* (Moving picture of Vienna) (1787), Johann Graf Fekete von Galantha wrote a special chapter on the masked balls and dances. "In the large hall people dance the minuet for several hours, as well as Contres and Germans in the Austrian manner. . . . In the suburbs there are an enormous number of dance halls. In addition, people dance at inns on Sundays and holidays all year round where the lowliest people try to forget the exhaustion of the week by clumsily hopping about."

We can imagine how lively these affairs were if we consider that during Maria Theresa's reign masked balls were under police supervision. The chastity commissions were kept busy. The most famous dance hall in Vienna except the Mehlgrube was the Casino on the Trattnerhof, later in the Augarten. On August 25, 1784, Count Zinzendorf wrote in his diary: "Soiree in the Augarten. I saw the Contre danced by 16 couples, all the men in blue, the women in white with blue hats and ribbons. The Prince of Wurttemberg danced Germans with my niece." The balls of the Court and of the nobility were given in the small *Redoutensaal*. Their Majesties attended those "Chamber Festivals" with or without masks; but the nobility gave private balls also in the Mehlgrube, where one could appear either masked or unmasked. There were balls for "Honest company," "distinction balls" for merchants and office workers (gentlemen paid one ducat in gold) and "closed companies" with certain regulations. The *Redoutensäle* were in the right wing of the Hofburg, on the side of the Josephplatz. This had been originally the place of a theater where opera and ballets were performed for the Court on festive occasions.

After the completion of the Burgtheater (1752) this place was rebuilt into the two *Redoutensäle* where Court festivities, public balls and masked balls were given. Masked balls took place on every Sunday during Carnival, as well as on Shrove Thursday, Sunday, Monday and Tuesday. Joseph II championed such public entertainment as a democratic way for the

111

various social classes to mix. He himself often put in an appearance, masked and incognito—another Harun al Raschid. Access to the hall was by carriage or sedan chair; admission was one ducat. In contrast to Venice, one was not permitted to wear masks on the street; offenders were arrested.

In addition, there existed a number of private dance halls, such as the de Franz'sche (or Hassen) House on Kaerntnerstrasse, the Stampfische "Summer" House on Tuchlauben, the large hall in the Waffenbergische House on Petersfreihof. Those balls, with "well-equipped music" and choice food and drink, were announced regularly in the "Vienna Diary." Finally, in 1787, Philip Otto, a tailor, founded a Casino in the Spiegelgasse, where, according to "Jahrbuch der Tonkunst in Wien und Prag" (1796), "balls were given during the Carnival, attended by clerks, merchants and other well-to-do people." Admission was so high that plebeians stayed away. "Females gratis," the announcements said, and characteristically, "Beginning: 6 P.M., end: never." The orchestra was about 40 pieces which had formed their own guild. Joseph II dissolved the organization and afterward the dance musicians met every Saturday morning behind the column on the Hohen Markt, ready for anybody who wanted to hire them.

Franz Graeffer (See Gugitz: *Wiener Memoiren und Wiener Dosenstuecke,* Munich 1918), the imaginative Vienna chronicler, lists a number of other dance halls which were en vogue during Mozart's time or immediately thereafter. "The Golden Pear" was one of the oldest and best known inns on Landstrasse and also a popular dance hall. The house was rebuilt in 1801 (originally it hadn't been more than a beer hall) and the neighboring house received a dance hall, "Wiener Annentempel," which was still frequented by Beethoven. Graeffer also mentions the Casino in the Trattnerhof where all kinds of important people and many aristocrats met; it combined library, coffeehouse, restaurant, dance hall. At 1 P.M. meals were served for 30 kreutzer, at 2 P.M. for one gulden, at 9:30 P.M. for 20 kreutzer. Musical amateurs could use the instruments which happened to be there, and paid nothing for light. During Carnival, balls took place weekly; otherwise monthly. Ball subscriptions cost 1 ducat per month, 4 ducats for half a year, 6 ducats for a full year. A Herr von Fuellenbaum was the entrepreneur. Entertainment was decent, gay, lively, conversational.

We know that the Casino existed as early as 1784, for the *Wiener Zeitung* reported that year: "The Casino for the nobility and other persons of distinction, which was licensed with the consent of the highest authority, will be opened on July 20 in the Trattnerische Freihof on the Graben, fourth stairway, first floor."

Another restaurant with a dance floor was the Sperl. It was located in the Kleinen Sperlgasse in Leopoldstadt and derived its name from the family Sperlbauer, original owners of the house in which had been a restaurant in the early 18th century. It was not until 1807, however, that the Sperl was rebuilt into a large dance hall and its days of greatness belong in the period before the revolution of March 1848, when Michael Pamer, Johann Strauss, Sr., and Lanner supplied the music for dance-happy Vienna. The glory of Sperl paled in the second half of the 19th century, since this dance hall, originally most distinguished, acquired a reputation for furthering prostitution.

Also, dances were held in many of the famous Vienna restaurants, even though there are no reports about actual dance entertainment. Mozart doubtlessly liked to patronize those beer halls and coffee houses, to have a glass of wine or a cup of coffee. Such places were the bourgeois beer hall *Zum goldenen Rebhuhn* (Golden Partridge), Goldschmiedgasse 632, which dates back to 1780; or the Tax' beer hall on Tuchlauben; or the *Tabakspfeife* (Tobacco Pipe), Goldschmiedgasse 618; the *Schwarzen Adler* (Black Eagle), *Weissen Roessel* (White Horse) both on Taborstrasse, and the Hotel *Goldenes Lamm* (Golden Lamb), Praterstrasse, where after 1635 the Turkish ambassadors lived; the *Zu den sieben Kurfürsten* (Seven Electors), Leopoldstadt, which existed as early as 1780, and which the poet Perinet liked to patronize. The restaurant, *Zum Derrfuss* was located in Jägerzeile, later Praterstrasse 472, and existed since 1780. The restaurant, *Zum schwarzen Tor* (Black Portal) was in the Rossau, in the ninth district, and was also mentioned as early as 1780. In Servitenstrasse nearby was the *Weisse Schwan* (White Swan) with a garden and 13 bowling alleys, and the *Goldene Schlange* (Golden Serpent) in the present Josephstaedter Haupstrasse, invited its patrons to good food and beer. Nearby was the *Goldene Ente* (Golden Duckling), and not far away, in the Alser suburb, the restaurant *Zur Elster* (Magpie). All those restaurants are mentioned in Graeffer's book, but the list is far from complete and does not contain the many suburban restaurants, beer halls, wine gardens where people danced the genuine popular dances which we may assume Mozart liked to watch when he had the chance. The folk dances were mostly *laendler* or dances resembling the *Ländler,* such as the *Fuerizwenger,* the *Kniebohrer,* the *Ummisteiger.* According to Richard Wolfram's *Die Volkstaenze in Oesterreich* (Austrian folk dances), the *Fuerizwenger* is characterized by a big step with the right foot; the left foot follows. The *Viertwenger Taenze* were mentioned as early as 1769 (according to the same source); the name deriving from *Furtwaenger* or *Furtwaengler,* which was the 17th century designation of the lumber carters of Lower and Upper Austria.

Our information about the popular dancing in the Vienna suburbs and the plains surrounding it, derives from statistical researches ordered by Archduke Johann. Richard Wolfram has discussed them in the pamphlet for Viktor Geramb. A report from Münichhofen near Ilz, dated 1811, says that the Styrian-rural and German dances were accompanied by first and second violins, bass with flute and cymbal. There was no viola; this probably was the reason why Mozart and other composers never used this instrument in his social dances. Also dated 1811, a report from Hetzendorf names as the usual dance instruments the violin, the violone, and the cymbal. Another report, from Goess, tells the Archduke: "The melodies derive from the well-known gliding dances from Styria. The local dances are generally known under the name of Styrian. Also, it is a characteristic that the dancers sing little songs in which they reveal their friendship, love or hostility toward one another; those dances are linked by variegated figures resembling the Strassburg."

A report from Neuberg, in the Mürz valley, is even more characteristic. "After harvest time, from about October 1 until advent, the 'little Carnival' takes place. During this period, the servants dance every Sunday until 10 o'clock at night, if the innkeeper permits. Every boy whose girl has trimmed his hat all summer long, on every Sunday and holiday, with small sprigs of carnations and violets, takes her to the dance. The crowds are so large that the floor allows barely less than two feet per pair. Every boy has the ambition to get enough space for his girl, but they respect the law of equality sufficiently to avoid quarrels and brawls unless provoked by visiting apprentices or other dancers who claim priority. No other dances are chosen except the provincial dance of Upper Styria, which resembles the Strassburgish. The music consists of one or two violins and a large or small cymbal. After 15 or 30 minutes, depending on the generosity of the musicians, the music stops and the dancers have to pay up. Every dancer must throw a kreutzer into the cymbal—and it is admirable how quick some of them manage to leave the hall so that it gets almost empty or occupied by girls. As the music resumes, it fills again in no time. The first violinist remembers those who vanished suddenly and when they want to disappear again during the next intermission, he claims his pay publicly. The girls get refreshments from the boys, wine and rosolio."

When Mozart was in Prague in 1787, he and Count Canal attended the so-called Bretfeld Ball, which took place on January 15. "This would have been something for you," he wrote to his Viennese friend, Gottfried von Jacquin. "I can see you run after all the beautiful girls and women—or rather, limp after them. I didn't dance and I didn't flirt; the first, because I was too tired, the second, because of my stupidity. But I watched with pleasure as all those people happily leaped and jumped to the music of my Figaro turned into contre dances and Germans. Because here nobody talks about anything but *Figaro*. Nothing gets played, sung, whistled but *Figaro*."

Actually, those balls were nationally famous. The following was written by Alfred Meissner, who allegedly based his imaginative *Rococobilder,* on notes by his grandfather, Gottlieb August Meissner, who knew Mozart. "The balls of Baron Bretfeld were famous for years. Anyone of rank, beauty, wealth, or talent, was invited. In two halls of medium size were the tables and the buffets."

Johann Baron Bretfeld von Kronenburg died in 1820. He was a lawyer and Professor of Law at the University, an exceptionally ambitious and versatile man who entertained lavishly and gave many huge balls.

At his home, the nobility and bourgeoisie of the Bohemian capital met every Thursday for 1 gulden admission, and there still exists a ticket for three Thursday balls in 1793, with an engraving featuring a scene and quotation from *Magic Flute*: "It jingles so softly, it jingles so clear." The dates on this ticket confirm the statement of Mozart who arrived in Prague on Thursday, January 11, and rode to the ball at 6 p.m. sharp. Manuscripts found in the library of the Bohemian National Museum enable us to see what kind of German dances were danced to *Figaro* melodies in 1787. A volume of popular airs and dances by Wolanek, Suessmayer, etc., contains not only *balli tedeschi*, melodies of a singspiel by Müller, *Die Schwestern von Prag* edited by the Czech violinist Wolanek, but also the famous *Figaro* dances which Mozart mentioned: they were called "*Balli tedeschi*, 1787." The date appears on the first page of the manuscript. The editor of those twelve German dances which end with a Coda, was either Johann Kanka, or his father, also a musically gifted man. Among the gentlemen who looked after Mozart during his first visit to Prague was Johann Count Pachta; according to Nissen, Mozart wrote "Nine contre dances with trio" on his request. The story goes that the music-loving Count asked Mozart repeatedly, but vainly, for this favor until he tricked him into writing them on the very day of a ball. The Count asked Mozart to dinner, but told him that they would be eating an hour earlier than usual; when Mozart arrived he found no dishes or food on the table, but only an inkwell, a pen and music paper. He is said to have written those contre dances within an hour. However, the dances usually connected with this anecdote (K.510) were found not to be by Mozart. The autograph is not in Mozart's handwriting, and the dances were probably written by some local musician. The incident in Pachta's palace, which Nissen relates, might well concern the 6 German dances (K.509). Count Pachta was one of the most highly cultured gentlemen in Prague. According to a letter which Count Max Lamberg, of Brünn, wrote in 1788 to Casanova, then in Dux, he was amiable and of good stock. "Ever since I lived in Prague, I was in silent awe of anybody that carried the name of this highly respectable family which boasted the most attractive qualities of the world." According to notes in the Casanova archives, Mozart probably met Casanova at Pachta's house. At a supper party in 1787, the Venetian adventurer was asked "to show his talent by improvising a piece of poetry in homage of the hostess." Casanova refused to comply, but on the following day sent the lady a poetic dedication of 64 lines. One year later, on March 17, 1788, her name day, Casanova sent her a poem and signed it, characteristically, "Deserted by the entire world except by love." As we know, Casanova was present at the world premiere of *Don Giovanni* in Prague on August 28, 1787, and even tried to write a new version for the sextet in the second act. The fact that he came to Count Pachta's house shows the relationship between those two representatives of the Rococo in a new and different light.

However, let's resume discussion of the dance halls of Prague, which Mozart must have known. A completely unknown booklet of 1748 reveals: "The conversation of two masks—a nobleman and a domino—about advantages and disadvantages of

Carnival balls and of how you have to behave while attending them." The Wussin Ball was the gathering place of local high nobility; one had to pay three gulden for a mask, and food included the famous "Oglio" soup, pastries, frozen berries—anything one could desire. At Kunze's Ball you paid only two gulden, in the *Engelsgarten* in the old district only 30 kreutzer. There you found a "Company of the best musicians who could cheer up the depressed mood of a melancholy person." The same may have applied to the ball in the Platteiser house; Mozart and Da Ponte lived there in the vicinity for a short time People then still danced the Minuet with a variety of masks—girls disguised as natives of the Tyrol or Augsburg, as gardners, even as bats. The booklet tells us that German dances were also used, but a domino made the statement that "The German dancing does not suit me, I consider it hard labor and try to avoid it."

The Materials for the old and new statistics of Bohemia, which appeared at Kaspar Wittman in Prague, in 1788, report about professional dance instruction. According to regulations, the guild of dancing masters in Prague recognized only dances like the *Pastorelle*; the *Prager Marionette*; *Menuett Demur*; *Paspje wandri*; *Madlot fransa*; *Laschursch*. Only one dance was blacklisted: the Waltz. The professional dancing masters loathed it, for it had dethroned the king of all dances, the Minuet; and the 150 pages of detailed analysis of its movements and gestures in *The Perfect Dancing Master,* had become superfluous. Therefore, it is not surprising that Johann Georg Jacobi, Goethe's friend and the author of Iris (1775) addressed all honorable men as follows: "We should not permit our wives, and daughters and sweethearts to be tossed about to the sounds of wild music, embraced by the arms of strangers, breast to breast with them and in complete abandon." But to spite the puritans and theoreticians, the big masses craved the waltz, screamed for the waltz.

It is not certain whether Mozart saw popular dancing in Prague. According to Czech sources, he visited the brother of his biographer Niemetschek in nearby Sadska. If this is correct, he must have become familiar with Czech popular music and popular dances. There are a few traces of Czech folk music in Mozart's works, however. On the contrary, the folk song which was just breaking into bloom, seems to have been influenced by Mozart. One example is the Czech national anthem *Kde domov muj*; the melody is identical with the main theme of the adagio of Mozart's *Sinfonia Concertante for Wind Instruments* (K.Anh. 9). In an article, "Mozart and the Czechs," in *Musical Quarterly*, of July, 1941, this author discussed the appearance of Mozart melodies in Czech folk music. But Mozart was familiar with Czech dances from early youth, and the 32nd piece in a notebook of the eight-year-old Wolfgang, dated London 1764, is a genuine Czech polka.

This notebook echoes the kind of popular music known to the Mozart family. In his book, "Bohemian National Dances"' (1859), the Bohemian historian, Alfred Waldau, described the various dances which were popular in the first half of the 19th century; we may assume that such dances were also used in Mozart's time, in the Bohemian countryside as well as in the suburbs of Prague. There were the *Strašák*, the *Okročák*, the *Kosaček*, the *Golubetz*, a.s.o., but, above all, the *Rejdovák* and the *Rejdovačka*; they stood in relationship of dance and afterdance, but in reverse order: the *Rejdovák* is a slow waltz, and its female counterpart a quick polka. Only a narrow step separates the *Rejdovačka* from Mozart's polka.

THE DANCES OF MOZART

Mozart began to write dances in his earliest youth. K.1, perhaps his "first" composition, was written when he was five or six years old. It was a Minuet and trio for piano. He continued to write minuets (K.2,4,5), and there are eight minuets in Leopold Mozart's notebook for Nannerl, 1759, in which he wrote that "Wolfgangerl" had learned them in his fourth year. The Minuet was the most popular form in those days, and was also used for instruction. The notebook for Nannerl also contains a "Menuet di Wolfango Mozart, d. 30 Novb. 1763 a Paris," which was included in K.7, a sonata for piano and violin in D Major; for contrast, Leopold added another Minuet, in D minor. The Minuet which Mozart interpolated in his Sonata K.9, in C Major, is worthy of notice. This Sonata, as well as K.8, was dedicated to the "stuffy and fastidious" Countess de Tessé, a lady in waiting of the Dauphine. The first Minuet anticipates the famous theme in A Major (K.331) which has a certain similarity with the South German folksong "Be glad my Heart, Think of no Pain." It appears in a South German (Ostracher) manuscript and dates from the early part of the 18th century. If we consider that the theme appeared for the first time in 1764, in Paris, and was used again, also in Paris, fourteen years later, we wonder whether the melody wasn't one of those international phenomena which traveled all over the continent; for it also appeared as a Czech folksong, *Hořela Lípa* (A lindentree burned).

In Mozart's London notebook of 1764, appear a number of Minuets, such as K.15-c and K.15. But the book also contains

120

counter dances, an Allemande, a Gigue, and, as already mentioned, a Polka.

Master Mozart, aged 8 or 9, also composed symphonies while in London. But while he used Minuets in his Sonatas—such as in K.19-d, which may be the first Sonata ever written for four hands—his early symphonies contain no Minuets. Not until he came to Vienna and heard the symphonies of Wagenseil, Monn, Starzer and other Viennese composers, did he place a Minuet, mostly with a contrasting trio, between the slow and the final movements.

It is significant that the Minuet became an essential part of that early Vienna symphony, for the "Vienna" symphonies of those pre-classical masters, which also included the youthful Haydn, largely depended on the divertimenti, cassations, serenades which were popular in Austria and had retained elements of the old suite. K.45 has a Minuet which was simply omitted when the symphony was used as the Overture for the opera buffa, *La Finta Semplice*. In general, Mozart used two or three part Minuets in his symphonies, the difference being that the three part form repeats the theme in the tonic, after a brief excursion into the dominant. K.112 and 113 are characteristic of the two part Minuet; a good example for the three part Minuet is in the *Haffner Symphony*, K.385. The latter, incidentally, is a typical "festive" Minuet, since it was originally used in a serenade written for a festivity at Sigmund Haffner's house in Salzburg, perhaps on occasion of his ennoblement. The festive spirit of the Minuet lies primarily in the large triad intervals and in the accent on the second beat in the second part of the Minuet. It is strange that the bucolic character of the triad intervals, which derived from the wide, uninhibited steps of the old *Weller* and the yodlers, eventually acquired aristocratic and bourgeois features. The trios, such as the one in the *Haffner Symphony*, are more linear and lyrical in comparison. Those trios are also in two or three parts. The Minuet in the *Linz Symphony* has the same festive character, this time emphasized by a dotted eighth; the trio resembles a Ländler. The Symphony K.504 in D Major, which Mozart wrote for performance in Prague on January 19, 1787, has no Minuet; the reason might be that the Italian tradition prevailed in the Bohemian capital. At any rate, in his Symphony in E-flat Major, K.543, Mozart returned to the festive Minuet with its wide intervals and emphatic ¾ beats, and he remained faithful to the Minuet until his last symphony, the *Jupiter*. In the sonatas, Mozart used the Minuet far more sparingly. The symphony was influenced by the suite and aimed at a wide audience which wanted to be amused, while the sonata aimed at a small, selected circle to which the entertainment value of the Minuet had little meaning. The essential feature of the Minuet was its formalism and it was meant to provide a quiet moment preceding the emotion of the finale. In Mozart's ballroom Minuets, the viola is always omitted; in this respect those dances have strange similarities with the sonatas for organ. The viola was no dance instrument, and the original dance band consisted of two violins and bass. Therefore, the scoring for strings, at once reveals whether a Minuet was written for a symphony or for the dance hall. Even the dances for large orchestra, with flutes, oboes, bassoons, trumpets and percussion instruments, have only two violins and bass.

Mozart's first ballroom minuets were K.65-a, seven minuets for two violins and bass, which he wrote in Salzburg in 1769. They deviate from the customary 32-bar structure, and still resemble the older form of the late Baroque period. During Carnival 1769, Mozart wrote 19 Minuets (K.103), with slightly stronger scoring, for two violins and bass, plus oboes and either two trumpets or two horns. Next came K.104 with six Minuets and Trio, K.105, also with six Minuets; K.61-g with two, K.61-h with six Minuets. Evidently, Mozart wrote a number of dances for the Carnival season; among them are K.64, a dance in wide intervals, scored for two violins, bass, and two horns, and, therefore, not meant for symphony. With K.123 (73-g) Mozart started his series of contre dances; it is scored for two oboes.

two horns, two violins and bass, and was written on April 13 or 14, 1770, in Rome. Leopold sent it to Salzburg with detailed choreographic instructions: "Wolfgang...sends a contre dance. He desires Mr. Cirillus Hofmann to invent the appropriate steps; when the two violins play the introduction only two dancers should lead the dance. Then, every time when the entire band plays with all the instruments, the entire group should dance together; it would be best to have five pairs of dances. The first pair could start the first solo, the second pair the second solo, and so on, because there are five soli and five tutti." These instructions of Mozart remind us of the old Baroque models, such as a ballet in Schoenbrunn, in 1670, to which Johann Heinrich Schmelzer composed the dances; three different groups of instruments were assigned to centaurs, nymphs, forest gods, and did not play together unless all the three dance groups danced simultaneously.

In his letter to his sister, dated April 21, Mozart mentioned this Contre dance and a Minuet which LePick is said to have danced in Milan. Mozart had sent the Minuet from Bologna to Salzburg, and it was probably K.94, introduced as Piano Piece No. 5 in Series XII. But a third part, added in the second bar of the second part, and with no pianistic features, seems to indicate the ballroom character of this dance. In Bologna, Mozart also composed a Minuet (K.122) without trio for two violins and bass, which, again, points to its use in the ballroom.

In the middle of December 1771, Mozart returned from Italy to Salzburg, and became seriously ill. Also, conditions in Salzburg had drastically changed. On December 16, Archbishop Sigismund von Schrattenbach, who had never objected to the concert tours of the Mozarts, had died and on March 14, 1772, Hieronymous Count Colloredo, Bishop of Gurk, became his successor.

We don't know for which occasion Mozart wrote the six Minuets K.164, dated June 1772; the autograph was later owned by Clara Schumann, and she might have given it to Brahms. A year later, in December, he wrote 16 Minuets with

Trio, K.176, for two violins, bass, two oboes, two horns and bassoon; oboes and horns can be replaced by flutes and trumpets. Strangely enough, none of these dances have been printed —parts of the autographs are in the Paris Conservatory, other parts with Mrs. Margarete Hummel in Florence, yet others with other private owners. Usually Mozart wrote series of six or twelve dances, following the practice of the old suite, which also may have a connection with the system of six workdays per week and the general principle of the hexagesimal system, such as presenting a lady with either six or 12 roses. In his edition of Köchel, Einstein emphasized that Mozart was considering a new organization of the dances in the suites. According to Einstein, the entire opus existed in a piano version, fragments of which have been preserved; the sixth Minuet, with slight revisions, appears already in the first Minuet of the Divertimento K.131. This was probably a collection of dances from different works which he originally used for his lessons, then orchestrated for dancing. In those days, such dance collections were frequent. Also, popular operatic arias were transcribed for piano. One of many examples in the treatment of *Figaro* melodies, by Johann Kanka, of Prague, was called the *Balli Tedeschi* 1787. Another example are five laendler for Josepha Gall which Einstein mentioned. It is not certain who Josepha Gall was; she may have been the daughter of a Salzburg woman, Therese Gall, who later married the beer brewer, Schlamb. In the collection of Mozart's Serenades, there is Serenade No. 2, subtitled Contre-dance, for two violins, two oboes (flute, bassoon), two horns, and bass; it consists of four movements (K.101). As Einstein wrote, the manuscript bore the title "Contredanse" and dates to the Carnival of 1776; this refutes original opinion that the piece was a serenade. Far more likely, it was a pantomimic presentation; the first dance, in four parts, was based on a very popular theme:

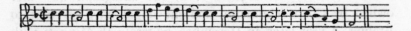

If we bear in mind what Leopold wrote from Rome on April 14, 1770, we can understand that even here, where the two violins play alone, a *pas de deux* was possible. The second part emphasizes the pantomimic element even more, because of the strong contrast of a sentimental *andantino* accompanied by pizzicato, and a spirited *allegro* melody. The two other dances are again in several parts and probably allow for any number of repetitions. That these dances were for the ballroom and not for serenading is proven by the fact that Mozart either omitted the viola or did not write it in.

With those dances, Mozart started the series of contre dances. Until then he had written almost exclusively ballroom Minuets. This can easily be understood. As he matured, he became greatly interested in social activities and entertainment, and the contre dance, with its many rounds and cotillions, promised better diversion than the stiff Minuet.

Like K.101, the four contre dances, K.267, are in different keys. They were written during Carnival of 1777, Wolfgang's last unclouded year in the parental household. In 1775, a large hall and several rooms were added to the City Hall of Salzburg, and during Carnival masquerades were held there, under the supervision of the magistrate. Mozart liked to dance and frolic. After a pastoral letter of May 14, 1779, Archbishop Colloredo prohibited any hocus-pocus and objectionable masquerading at passion plays and processions; so probably people tried to counterbalance the graveness of Passion-week with some fun and amusement during Carnival. (See Mayr in his sketch about Archbishop Colloredo, 18. *Programm des Staatsgymnasiums in Salzburg.*)

However, Mozart had not abandoned the Minuet. In 1780, according to Einstein's chronology, he wrote three Minuets without a trio, for two violins, bass, oboes, bassoons, horns, high trumpets, and kettledrum (K.363). As compared to the scoring of the later Vienna dance series, the flutes and clarinets are missing. The horns and trumpets with percussion, which the Minuets introduced, indicate that they were written for a festive occasion, and the last Minuet in D-Major, with its knocking effect, reminds us of the Minuet in *Don Giovanni*. The next dances, K.461, already belong in Mozart's Vienna period. Six Minuets have two violins, bass, two oboes (Flutes), two bassoons, and two horns. The manuscript, which is partly in the Library in Berlin, partly in the Library of Congress, has a remark by Julius André, which reads: "The sixty is faulty. One can substitute the following Quadrille." Those dances show considerable progress over the preceding one. They are clever and more stylized than the contre dances. A certain stiffness is still evident, appropriate to the occasion for which they were written.

Another "American" manuscript is K.462, six Contre dances for two violins and bass. The originals are in the Newberry Library, in Chicago. Mozart later added oboes and horns, and wrote the wind part on two seperate sheets. The fact that he called them "Six Contredanses" for two violins and bass, indicates that he did not think in terms of a viola to augment the bass. At about the same time he wrote K.463, two Minuets with two Contredances interpolated; one Minuet and one Allegro are joined into a Quadrille. The second Minuet is called *Adagio Menuetto Cantabile*. The two dances, K.462 and 463, are closely connected, for the last page of the autograph is a sort of "letter in notes," in which Mozart writes, "Dear friend"; then follow 24 bars of the melody of the fifth contredance of K.462. It is possible that Mozart himself devised the choreography for those dances. We know that he attended the Bretfeld Ball in Prague; also, according to Nissen (Page 561) he had to write several contre dances for Count Pachta. It had been assumed that these were the nine contredances or Quadrilles which appear as K.510 in the old edition of Mozart's *Gesamtausgabe*; but, as I indicated in a report to a musicological convention of the Mozarteum in 1931, those dances could not possibly have been written by Mozart. The handwriting is completely different; it is a steep, conventional handwriting which does not correspond to Mozart's character; notes, pauses and key signatures are differently written; and there were errors in spelling, already mentioned by Nottebohm, such as "passo" instead of "basso," "Scinelli" instead of "Cineli." This would indicate that the composer spoke a German-Bohemian provincial dialect; the people of the Saxonian regions of Bohemia used to pronounce B like P, and vice versa, and said "Shinellen" for "Cinellen." "Oboe" was germanized into "oboa"; "timpano," contrary to Mozart's spelling, was written with a "y," and an *accent grave; da capo* had inverted accent. The brackets lack the little dashes characteristic of Mozart.

For the rest, one can recognize two different handwritings, two different sorts of ink. Certain words, like *Contra T* and *3. quadrigle* were written by someone else, possibly by Mozart. I have examined the manuscript, together with the graphologer, Broessler, who is familiar with Mozart's handwriting. He, too, thought that those words, which were added later, were written by Mozart. But by no means did Mozart write the entire manuscript. The handwriting is that of an older man of over fifty; also it was not written in a hurry, but leisurely, all of which would refute the Pachta legend.

In comparison with the German dances of Prague, which have the genuine Mozartean diction, the contre dances are completely un-Mozartean. This was already shown in a paper by Professor Becking, based on his method of tone analysis, which I added to my own paper given at a Mozart convention in Salzburg, in 1931. Many elements from folk and military music were taken over. The Quadrille in No. 1 has a trio which is part of a march in B-flat Major, the old Grenadier March, later also composed by Beethoven, for two clarinets, bassoons, horns. (Series 25, Supplement of the Collected Works No. 20), Contre Dance, No. 6 was also used by Beethoven, in an arrangement of the Grenadier March for flute, a work to which Kinsky drew our attention in an essay, "Beethoven and Flutework" in Bosse's Beethoven Almanac, 1927. This march has a long history; of which I only mention that Weber used the melody in his "Kampf und Sieg" as Austrian general march and that it was in use up to the 20th century, in Austrian military music as the trio of the Austrian regimental march No. 42.

No. 8, The Contredance *La Fenite,* was the melody of the old German dance, "Lott is Dead." Böhme's "History of the Dance in Germany," states that it was known since 1868, as "Manchester," and quick gallop. Actually, the tempo is indicated by the bowdlerized name of *fenite,* which should read, *fuite,* the quick part of the contre dance. This evidence of poor education proves that Mozart could not have been the composer. The Pyramide is very often the last part of the Quadrille.

The last Quadrille is awkward in style; its shallow sequences and short, insignificant themes are typical of the all too prolific writers of dance music toward the end of the 18th century.

If the contre dances stored at Prague University were not written by Mozart, the incident in Pachta's house may pertain to the Six German Dances, also written in Prague. They are for two violins, bass, two flutes, piccolo, two oboes, two clarinets, two bassoons, two horns, two high trumpets, kettledrum (K.509); Alfred Einstein shares this opinion. The autograph, at Berlin Staatsbibliothek, has the title, *6 Tedeschi di W. A. Mozart Praga 1787.*

According to Mozart's list, No. 51 are the dances which he wrote on February 6. A note at the end of the score leads us to believe that Mozart was not well acquainted with local orchestral conditions. "Each German dance has its trio, or rather *alternativo*; after this, the German is repeated, then again the *alternativo*; then follows a transition to the next German. Since I don't know what kind of piccolo is being used here, I write it in the natural key; it can always be transposed. Mozart."

Despite the emphasis on a popular style, those dances show a definitely festive atmosphere, indicating that they were meant for the Prague nobility. This is especially true of the first, third and sixth dance. No. 2 has the traditional grace notes which Abert mentions; they also occur in the German in the ballroom scene of *Don Giovanni.* For the rest, it seems to be a quotation from the aria, *Come un Agnello,* from Sarti's *Fra due Litiganti,* which was very popular in Prague and is also quoted in *Don Giovanni*.

But those dances are not only significant for the local history of Prague; they are equally important in Mozart's work. It seems that they whetted his appetite for dance music, for they are followed by a series of elaborate dances which, according to Einstein, "are completely different, in scoring and impact, from dances he had written earlier, in Salzburg."

Einstein mentions a copy of those dances, which contain six more Germans with trios and were performed in the small Redoutensaal in 1795. On January 14, 1788, he wrote, "Donnerwetter" (K.534), a contredance for two violins, bass, two oboes, two horns, piccolo and drum. Unfortunately, we have only a piano version of this short humoristic dance, which was written a few days after K.535 and also belongs in the group of Mozart's programmatic contre dances. We can't expect the technique and expressiveness of "Thunderstorm" to be on a level with Beethoven's *Pastoral Symphony* or the *Prometheus* music, and we can't even compare it with the "storms" of the French Baroque opera. Mozart's programmatic contre dances were probably meant to be humoristic; it is noteworthy that the waltz composers, especially Johann Strauss, adopted the idea.

Mozart's, *Bataille*, (K. 535) seems to belong in the category of the old *battaglie;* for in an old score at the *Gesellschaft der Musikfreunde* in Vienna it is called, "Die Eroberung von Belgrad." And in the *Wiener Zeitung* of March 19, 1788, it is announced under the same title. The first war of Joseph II against the Turks was declared on February 9, 1788. A siege of Belgrade was expected, did not take place. The conquest of Belgrade by Laudon occurred in 1789. It generated a series of "tone pictures," such as Ferdinand Kauer's *Le Siege de Belgrade;* others by Vincenz Maschek, F. J. Freystaettler, a.o. Mozart's *Bataille* is in four parts which end with a Turkish march, *Marcia Turca*. The Turkish character of the music is indicated by the use of a piccolo, to which are added clarinets, bassoon, trumpet, drum, and strings; it is also indicated by sharp grace notes, dotted eighths and a long cello trill on C.

Closely connected with the *Bataille* is K.587, *The Victory of the Hero Coburg*, quoting a marching song about the hero and his victory over the Turks on September 22, 1789. It has been said that Mozart meant to indicate the Turkish atmosphere by use of a theme in a minor key. The dance was written down in December 1789.

The hero was Field Marshal Friedrich Josias Coburg-Saalfeld (1737-1815) who, together with the Russians, scored decisive victories over the Turks, at Chotym, Fokschann and finally, at Martinesti. Mozart's contre dance seems to refer to the battle of Martinesti. It is, therefore, closely connected with Franz Christoph Neubauer's *Bataille de Martinesti oder Coburg's Sieg*, a tone picture for orchestra. Mozart's dance is more elaborate this time and even shows intricate thematic work. It seems that Mozart had definite aims as to its dedication. Three contre dances for orchestra, K.535-a, written in Vienna early in 1788, are little known and were not reprinted; so is the contre dance K.535-b, of which only a violin part exists. On January 27, Mozart wrote six Germans, K.536, for violins, bass, two flutes, piccolo, two oboes or clarinets, bassoons, horns, trumpets, and kettledrums. Those dances and K.567 were also published in piano score by Artaria & Co. and J. M. Goetz in Munich. Here, too, we find popular phrases or melodic fragments which were taken either from popular music or popular contemporary opera arias, songs or dances. Some of those dances have uncommonly wide intervals, such as in No. 4 and the Trio No. 5. No. 6 is undoubtedly identical with the melody *Com' un agnello* from Sarti's *Due Litiganti*. Also, Trio No. 6 contains a quotation from *Figaro*.

On October 30, 1788, he wrote two contre dances (K.565) which are mentioned in his autograph list as No. 99.

The Six German Dances K.567 were written on December 6, 1788, in Vienna; they are characterized by a Coda and variegated instrumentation of the individual dances. In No. 2, for example, the violins, horns, bassoons and clarinets are augmented by flute and kettledrum; No. 3 has piccoli, No. 4, oboes. The trio of No. 5 has a *tamburo*. The Coda returns to No. 6 and has a pompous upbeat, expanded by triplets; the main theme was taken from the preceding trio. I do not know from where Mozart derived the use of the Coda. Could he himself have been its originator? Later, with Lanner and Strauss, it assumed programmatic significance as the melodic summary of the dances; almost as in a dream, the dancers relive the preceding experience in concentrated form.

Only a few days after writing down K.567, on December 24, Mozart wrote 12 Minuets (K.568), which were obviously meant for the Carnival in the Redoutensälen. For those balls wrote composers like Haydn, Beethoven, Hummel, Koželuch, Maschek, etc. Those Minuets are more stylized than the German. The trio of the first dance is similar to a Variation in the Piano Sonata in A Major, which Mozart has also quoted elsewhere. Musically, those dances are on an exceptionally high level; some of them, i.e., No. 6, remind us of the *Don Giovanni* Minuet. The trio, in a minor key, with chromatically ascending phrases, is particularly appealing.

The year 1789 brought an especially large number of dance commissions. On February 21, Mozart wrote Six German Dances, K.571, which were meant for the small *Redoutensaal*, and were also played in the following year. These dances also have a Coda which, similar to the one in K.567, follows the last dance. It is introduced by an elaborate upbeat in the manner of a Mannheim crescendo, and continues by a chromatic sliding melody. Those dances reveal the great genius of Mozart, who can express more within the smallest frame than many others in an over-dimensional symphony. In December of the same year, he wrote 12 Minuets (K.585); and presented the manuscript to his friend, the conductor, Franz Roser (1779-1830), son of the musical director of the Cathedral at Linz, Johann Georg Roser von Reiter (1740-1784). Roser himself wrote on the first page of those dances: "Mozart wrote those

Minuets for two violins and basso, in 1789; but since they were received with so much success, Mozart was asked to give them a larger instrumentation; so he augmented the score and it is in his own handwriting and he gave it to me as a present two weeks before his death. Franz Roser." Incidentally, it was Roser who fulfilled the wish of the dying Mozart and sang to him the bird-catcher's song; and he was among the few who went to the funeral. At the same time, December 1789, Mozart wrote 12 German Dances, K.586, which, again, are characterized by the strong emphasis on the popular element, especially the ninth dance. In January 1790, followed K.106 (588-a). Those three contre dances for two violins, bass, two oboes, two bassoons, two horns are preceded by an "Overture," which, however, was called an *intrada*, in the sense of the old suite. Those dances are in a category between serenades and dances. Maybe, also, the Overture was meant to give the dancers time to assemble after the dancing master had called them together.

Strangely enough, Mozart composed the greatest number of his dances in the year of his death. The reason may be that frequent illness and destitution forced him to produce as much as possible. The Six Minuets, K.599, were written on January 23, for the "Redoute." The *Wiener Zeitung* ran an announcement in December: "W. A. Mozart: 12 Redouten Minuets with all the parts," which means that Mozart wrote those dances for publication by Artaria only with two violins and bass, and added the wind parts later. The same is true of Six German Dances, K.600, which he wrote on January 29. Here he added a piccolo in the trio of the fifth dance; together with the first violin, it was supposed to imitate a canary. On February 5, he wrote Four Minuets, K.601. In the trio of the first dance, in B-flat Major, we recognize a similarity with the *Don Giovanni* minuet; altogether, those minuets sound rather pompous. On the same day he wrote Four Germans, K.602, and Two Contre dances, K.603. There is no doubt that those dances, K.600 through K.607, had been commissioned at the same time. Some of them, such as K.601, 602, and 603, were written on the same day and probably in one sitting. In the trio of the second dance of K.601, Mozart added a piccolo and a lyre; the hurdy-gurdy was a popular instrument in those days, and Baton, Chedeville, Pleyel and Haydn wrote music for it. (See Sachs, *Reallexikon der Musikinstrumente*.) The use of this popular instrument by Mozart indicates that he may have used a melody that was the rage in Vienna just then; which the hurdy-gurdy bass fits completely. Compare the melody of the second part of this trio with *Halter zu Pentzing*, which Alfred Orel took from

Hafner's collection, *Scherz und Ernst in Liedern*.

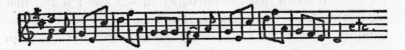

In K.605 of Three Germans dated February 12, the famous sleighride appears as the trio of the third dance; we must remember that such sleighrides were known at the Vienna court already in the 17th Century. With bells and fanfare people rode out to the suburbs or to the Prater. In the sleighride-Trio Mozart also used two postilion's horns which also appear in the Coda. His father, Leopold, had also written such a sleighride. The melody of Wolfgang's sleighride can be found in Schottky's folksong collection of 1819, as a burden of the song, *Weltlauf*.

On Page 132 of his book, "Wolfgang Amadeus Mozart," Robert Haas reproduced a New Year's card from Old Vienna showing the sleighride-Trio for two violins and cello. The first violin part is at the top, the second to the left, the cello part to the right. This card probably was an invitation to a private ball, comparable to the Bretfeld balls of Prague. Musical sleighrides were first written by Johann Heinrich Schmelzer in the 17th century.

We still have to mention Six Laendler (K.606), which were originally scored for orchestra, but transposed by Mozart for two violins and bass. In his poem, *Der Steyrer Tanz*, Nikolaus Lenau gives a charming description of this lively, originally pantomimic, dance with its *tours de main* and clapping of hands. In none of his other dances did Mozart absorb the popular tone of the laendler to that extent, and it almost seems that a Styrian or Upper Austrian song was quoted in No. 3. These dances are direct forerunners of those of Schubert, Lanner, and Johann Strauss.

On February 28, Mozart composed his contre dances, *Trionfo delle donne*, K.607; however, only a fragment exists, since the autograph breaks off after the fourth page at Measure 53. Mozart used melodies from Pasquale Anfossi's *Il trionfo delle donne*, an opera buffa which was premiered in Vienna, on May 15, 1786. It seems that the introduction was also lost and that the contre dance was in six parts at least. As we know, in the banquet scene of *Don Giovanni*, Mozart used the *Non piu andrai* from *Figaro*, one of the most popular melodies in Prague. And, as mentioned, the Prague musician and lawyer, Kanka, used this melody, along with others, for his *Balli Tedeschi*, 1787. But Mozart also used the melody in Five Contre dances (K.609), scored for two violins, bass and flute (1791). Probably this version was written for a private ball where only a small orchestra was used. Dance No. 4 has three alternatives, which were played like couplets to the rondo theme in C-Major. No. 5 has the designation, *Die Leyerer*—and indeed, one can imagine the theme played by an organ grinder. On March 6 came the contre dances *Les Filles Malicieuses*, which is identical with the *Leyerer* of K.609, except that it uses horns in G. Since this dance was written down on March 6, there can be no doubt that K.609 was written at the same time. Why it was called *Les Filles Malicieuses* has found no explanation so far; contrary to Abert's opinion, it seems to be a programmatic piece, perhaps alluding to the daughters of the host or patron. On the same day, Mozart wrote a German, K.611, which, however, is identical with K.602. Here the trio is called *Leierer Trio* referring, of course, to the barrel-organ.

The dances enumerated here do not represent Mozart's entire work in this field. In Vol. 1 of *Zeitschrift für Musikwissenschaft*, Robert Lach published an unknown Minuet which he places at the beginning of the 1780's; and in Vol. 1 of the *Mozart Jahrbuch* (1923), Friedrich Frischenschlager wrote about six minuets which he placed in Mozart's early years. Mozart did not take the genre all too seriously, and occasionally wrote a few measures on any handy scrap of paper, for later use.

Mozart's genius was so universal that he was at home in all styles of composition which he knew: the galant style, the Rococo, the Sentimental, the Baroque, blend under the impact of his personality to his very individual style. It is significant that toward the end of his life he returned to the old Baroque style, to polyphonic, constructive writing, which he might have raised to an exalted new style, like Beethoven, had he lived. Gottfried van Swieten, one of the great patrons of music in Vienna, and imperial representative at the Prussian court between 1770 and 1777, was extremely interested in Bach and Handel. Frederick the Great had already given up music, and the custodian of musical tradition in Berlin was Princess Amalie, the King's sister, a typical lady of the old Prussian style. Even Gluck was too modern for her taste. She arranged musical afternoons, at which works in the old style were performed. Arneth's biography of Empress Maria Theresa contains a letter of van Swieten to Count Kaunitz, the powerful statesman, describing an audience with the King: "Among other things, he talked with me about music and a great organist named Bach, who happened to be in Berlin. This artist has great talent, according to all I hear or can imagine, tremendous knowledge of harmony and power of execution. Those who knew his father find that he does not measure up to him, however. The King shares this view, and to prove to me that he was right, he sang, in a loud voice, the theme of a chromatic fugue which he had given to the older Bach who immediately turned it into a fugue of 4, then 5, and finally 8 voices." This letter of course refers to J. S. Bach's "Musical Offering." Van Swieten apparently had heard little about Johann Sebastian Bach, but we may assume that the King's authority also in musical matters, made an overwhelming impression on the Austrian diplomat who had written in 1773, in Leyden, a doctor's thesis about the influence of music on medicine. From then on, van Swieten was the victim of a virtual Bachomania. When he returned to Vienna, he brought with him a great deal of music by Handel, Bach, and other Baroque composers. His enthusiasm carried Mozart along and after 1782, he developed a growing interest for the old style, perhaps also because his wife had a puzzling predilection for fugues. Mozart arranged for his patron, van Swieten, three fugues from the well-tempered Clavier, and one from Art of the Fugue, and he also wrote a piano suite, K.399, of which only the Overture, the Allemande, the Courante, and six bars of the Sarabande are preserved.

It is hard to say whether Mozart ended this piano suite with a Gigue, and perhaps interpolated a so-called Intermezzo, a Bouree or Gavotte, between the Sarabande and Gigue. The appealing feature of these belated compositions, the Overture and the dances, is the fact that Mozart first invented a Baroque melody, but then subordinated it to the laws of classical harmony while its rippling, curling phrases illustrate the freedom of his spirit. Triad melodies, parallel thirds and sixths reveal that he belonged to the galant age.

And so we close the dance rounds around Mozart. This modest piece of research has tried to show Mozart and his creative genius through his accomplishment in the field of the dance.

HAYDN

Long stretches of Haydn's life have not yet been explored. Biographies written by G. A. Griesinger, a Saxon diplomat; A. C. Dies, a painter; and Giuseppe Carpani, an Italian writer; as well as others based on Haydn's personal reminiscences are unreliable. Moreover, the memory of the aged composer was often inaccurate. Sometime in early childhood he beat the kettledrum in a church procession, and he already may have played for dances at his native village of Rohrau. In 1740, Kapellmeister J. G. Reutter discovered him and engaged him as a singer in the St. Stephen Convent in Vienna. When his voice broke he was dismissed and went back to the dance halls to make a living.

His symphonies and chamber music offer ample evidence of the important place the dance and dance rhythms occupied in his creative inspiration. He stylized dance melodies, which he had heard in early youth; but for the many balls and redoutes at the Esterházy Courts in Eisenstadt and Esterház, he composed dance music, as he had done in his previous position of musical director to Count Morzin, in Lukawetz.

As a Court Conductor at Esterház he also had to play at festivities in the neighboring capital of Pressburg (now Bratislava). Spectacular festivities took place on November 16, 1772, when Anton Count Grassalkovicz, Guardian of the Crown of Hungary, entertained the Hungarian governor, Duke Albert and his consort, Archduchess Maria Christine. Kapellmeister Haydn had been requested to conduct the dance orchestra. He probably wrote a greater number of dances than any other classical composer. Actually, most of the dances were not published until the 1780's and 1790's; among them are the *Raccolta de Menuetti Ballabili*, written in 1784, published by Artaria. The *Wiener Zeitung*, announcing their publication, wrote that Haydn had not had any dance Minuets printed in 12 years. Those dances—similar to Mozart's dance Minuets—were scored for two violins, bass, flute, two oboes, bassoon, two horns and kettledrums, but no violas. Some have the grace notes *alla Lombarda* (Scotch Snap), which were characteristic of the popular dance music of the time and still used by Lanner and Strauss.

On October 13, 1806, when Haydn's biographer, Griesinger, introduced the author and book dealer, Friedrich Justin Bertuch, to the aged composer, the latter promised Bertuch a concise survey of his compositions; he gave it to him on November 20. The last item on the list was, "Minuets und Teutsche—400."

In Vol. I of Anthony van Hoboken's thematic bibliographic list of Haydn's works, there are no fewer than 285 dances: 212 are minuets, 59 German, 8 Zingarese, 5 Quadrille, 1 English. It is hardly possible to ascertain whether or not all those dances are authentic, since in those days publishers liked to issue dances under some famous name. Haydn's first dance compositions, 16 Minuets, were published, in manuscript copy, by Breitkopf; but Hoboken lists 12 earlier minuets.

In 1787, Haydn wrote 6 German dances, published by Artaria and entitled *Six Allemandes à Plusieurs Instrumens*. Their melodies are based on a triad in typical alpine fashion. More dances existed but were lost; among them are 12 Minuets which Haydn wrote for Prince Kraft Ernst von Oettingen-Wallerstein, on the occasion of the Prince's marriage with Wilhelmine Friderike, daughter of Duke Eugen Ludwig of Württemberg, on October 12, 1789. However, the dances arrived too late. Haydn would have liked to see them in print; on January 11, 1790, he wrote to Artaria about his "splendid, new minuets with 12 trios," and charged the price of 12 ducats. But Artaria did not print them.

One of the most popular dance halls in Vienna was the *Re-*

douten Säle. In 1792, Haydn composed 12 Minuets for balls which were held there, and Artaria had them transcribed for piano. Artaria also published a reduced arrangement for *Bauern-besetzung*—rustic band (two violins and bass) in 1794. Those masked balls were later called *Katharina-Redouten*, after St. Catherine who has her nameday on November 25. Catherine of Alexandria is the patron saint of philosophers and has been glorified in many works of art; for this reason the "Gesellschaft bildender Künstler in Wien" chose her as the patroness of those balls which were held for the benefit of its *Witwen-Institut* (the widows of its members).

The announcement of the masked ball of 1792 said that, "out of love for the kinship of the arts, and for the benefit of the Committee, the famous Kapellmeister, Joseph Haydn, has written original music for the minuets and German dances."

Haydn returned to Vienna in June 1792. It is not certain whether he attended any of those festivities, but the early 19th century author, Franz Graeffer, who wrote about a masked ball states that this was the case. In his memoirs, Graeffer introduced Haydn, who had just returned from London, in a fictitious conversation with his old friend, Field Marshal Franz Graf von Lacy (1725-1801).

As the summary shows, Haydn's dance music centered on the Minuet. There are comparatively few German dances and Quadrilles. Haydn, Mozart's senior by nearly a generation, still belonged to the age of the Minuet.

From Hoboken's listing, we can see that Haydn was also interested in gypsy music. Among the eight *Zingarese* for piano, No. 8 is a good example of the "gypsy scale" with the augmented fourth, which Liszt was to use in his Hungarian Rhapsodies. The scholar of folklore, Frantisek S. Kuhač, has found that Haydn derived numerous themes from Croatian folk songs, and, as a result, the English writer, W. H. Hadow has dubbed Haydn a Croatian composer.

Actually, there may have been Slavs or Hungarians among

Haydn's ancestors; part of the population around Hainburg and Rohrau is of mixed stock. However, as early as 1909, the French musicologist, Michel Brenet wrote in the Courrier Musical (*A propos du centenaire de Haydn*) that the similarity of Haydn melodies with Croatian folksongs should not cause us to jump to conclusions, least of all about the composer's national origin. Just the opposite: it has been claimed that classical music had a decisive influence on the development of folk music, including the Czech and Croatian. The Czech musicologist, Vladimir Helfert, has proved that the Czech folksong, a product of the 18th century, was largely derived from contemporary Italian and German music. Take, for instance, a song, *Hořela, lipa, hořela,* which J. Erben in his collection of Czech folk songs: *České písné a řikadla* (Prague, 1836). Undoubtedly, it stems from the variation theme of the piano sonata in A Major (K.331) by Mozart, who probably became acquainted with it through a song in the *Ostracher Liederhandschrift* (early in 18th century).

Haydn no doubt was interested in Hungarian folk music. In 1802, he even wrote a "Hungarian National March," for trumpet, 2 oboes, 2 clarinets, 2 bassoons and 2 horns. On September 28, 1802, he wrote to the oboist, Jakob Hyrtl that his copyist Elssler (the grandfather of Fanny Elssler) would bring him a new military march, and he gave detailed directions for a possible simplification of the oboe part. Pohl believes that Haydn may have written the march as the counterpart to the Austrian national anthem, or perhaps in honor of the Russian Prince who visited Prince Esterhazy later in October.

Szabolcsi's article, "Joseph Haydn and Hungarian Music," lists the Hungarisms in Haydn's music. The author points out that part of those melodic similarities belong to so-called *Verbunkos-Musik* (around 1800), and are, therefore, *pseudo*-Hungarian—in contrast to Bartok's peasant music which is *genuinely* Hungarian. The Symphony No. 104, in D-minor, (the seventh London Symphony), comes to mind; its finale was known in 18th century Bohemia as Okročak.

Haydn also resorted to Hungarian, Slavic and Austrian folk music. An example is the Capriccio for piano (Hoboken XVII, No. 1) based on an old *Ländler*.

The text being as follows:

> Eahna achte muessen's sein,
> Wann s'an Saubarn wolln schneidn.

The manuscript, which is owned by Mrs. Gisella Selden-Goth, of Florence, Italy, has the following title:

"Capriccio Acht Sauschneider mussen seyn del Giuseppe Haydn, mpria 764."

The song was also sung to the text, "Ich wollt' es wäre Nacht" (I wish it were night). In "Notenbüchlein für Nannerl Mozart" which Leopold wrote for his young daughter, we find a Scherzo by Wagenseil, which uses the same tune.

It also appears in Mozart's *Galimathias Musicum* (K. 32). The Ländler obviously was one of Haydn's favorite melodies, for he used it also in his String Quartet Op. No. 6; this proves that both Haydn and Mozart used popular melodies, which were danced as Ländler and hop waltzes, in the minuets of their symphonies and quartets.

Haydn's famous *Ochsen-Menuett* ("oxen" minuet) deserves special discussion. The title of this brief work derives from the anecdote that a butcher ordered a minuet from Haydn for the wedding of his daughter, for the fee of a beautifully adorned ox. One of the many editions of

this minuet

with the trio

featured a lithographic illustration of the incident. One copy, in the monastery of Goettweig (Hoboken) features a picture of Haydn's residence in Gumpendorf; the composer stands at the window; in front of his house crowds have gathered around the butcher with the ox and many musicians with clarinets and horns. Strangely, none of the early Hadyn biographies mention this anecdote; Griesinger even doubts its authenticity. As late as 1897, Ditson, in New York, published "Haydn's Celebrated Oxen- Waltz," arranged by J. S. Knight; the title page shows two dancing oxen. Ignaz von Seyfried used the incident in his Singspiel, as *Ochsenmenuett* (The Oxen-Minuet) which was given for his benefit at the Theater an der Wien, on December 13, 1823. One year earlier, a vaudeville by Hoffmann, *"Haydn ou les Menuets du Boeuf,* had been performed in Paris. Seyfried's Singspiel has been reissued in our own day and has had various performances.

BEETHOVEN

In contrast to the jovial Mozart for whom play and dance were necessities of life, Beethoven, though he was no Puritan, but cherished high-flown ideals, had an aversion against all too mundane pleasures. Shortly after his arrival in Vienna he took some lessons with the dancing master, Lindner, whose name appears in his oldest sketch book, but he did not really like to dance. That he took dancing and riding lessons shows his ambition to move as an equal among the Viennese aristocrats. We don't know whether or not he had an opportunity in Bonn to visit balls; there exist no dance compositions from his Bonn period, but he wrote the music for a *Ritterballet* which was performed on Sunday, March 6, 1791.

This *Ritterballet* (equestrian ballet) is among the few vestiges of the old tournament ballets, which can be traced to the tournaments of the Middle Ages, in which music played an important part. The descriptions of tournaments in the various "Cartels", usually specified the number of "trumpets", meaning all kinds of wind instruments. In the course of the centuries, the tournament was glorified, entered the realm of aesthetics, and became a theatrical act of allegorical nature. Their French name was courses de testes. Their last offshoot, the merry-go-round, may be a good example of the *gesunkenes Kulturgut*.

In Italy, the dramatic allegorical tournaments—*Balletti a cavallo*—occupied a very important place. Equestrian ballets were performed at practically all the German courts, and the most famous were those performed in Vienna, on occasion of the marriage of Emperor Leopold I to Marguerite of Spain, in

143

1667. Antonio Bertali wrote the vocal music for one of them, Marc Antonio Cesti for the other, and Johann Heinrich Schmelzer the dances for both. Bertali's music to *La Contesa del Aria e del Acqua* has been preserved, but that for Cesti's *La Germania Esultante* is missing; the dances are preserved for both. Similar festivities took place in Durlach, Dresden and Munich. In his *Gesprächspiele*, Philip Harsdörfer (1607-1658) told a great deal about theatricals on horseback and even published a six-part music for trumpets. While the tournaments of the Baroque were mostly accompanied by trumpets, Beethoven's *Ritterballet* was scored for strings and winds. He wrote it during the winter of 1790-91, in Bonn; H. Reichhard's *Theater-Kalender* (theater almanac) for 1792 features a report of this performance, which may have been written by Neefe, the most important tutor Beethoven had in Bonn: "On Shrove Sunday (March 6, 1791) the nobility performed in the *Redoutensaal* a 'characteristic ballet' in old-German costume. Its author, His Excellency Count Waldstein, who has done himself proud by the dance and the music, has considered our forefathers' predilections for warfare, hunting, love, and food. On March 8, the high nobility came to the theater in old-German attire; the procession was a big, resplendent spectacle, and it showed that the ladies would lose none of their charms if they would again choose to wear the garb of bygone days."

Ferdinand Ernst Count Waldstein (1762-1823) had come to Bonn in 1787 to go through the novitiate of the Teutonic Order (Deutscher Ritterorden). Maximilian Franz, Elector and Archbishop of Cologne, the youngest brother of Emperor Joseph II, was Grand-Master of the Teutonic Order the site of which was in Mergentheim, until he was summoned to Cologne in 1784. In 1791, Beethoven, then with the Bonn Court Orchestra, had gone there to attend the Convention of the Order.

The Order, which had its headquarters in Mergentheim since 1526, had 12 "provinces." It derived from the Orders created during the Crusades, and in Beethoven's time it had purely social significance. Count Waldstein, who was exceptionally important in Beethoven's life since he sent him to Vienna, and to whom the famous Waldstein Sonata Op. 53 is dedicated, was a Knight of the Order, and it may be assumed that he wanted to arrange a medieval tournament for the past Grand Master and the nobility. Wegeler says in his, "Biographical Notes about Beethoven" that Count Waldstein arranged the choreography with the assistance of dancing master Habich, of Aachen. The Count was also considered the composer, since Beethoven had not revealed his authorship and thus became a kind of ghostwriter for Waldstein. The above-mentioned Gotha Theater Almanac explicitly names Waldstein as the composer. It might be that the melodies, or some of them, were invented by the Count; they are melodically weak. Thayer (Vol. 1, page 308) says that the ballet also had vocal parts. A sheet of such vocal music was sold by auction in London around 1910; Eduard Speyer, the well-known London collector, had seen it and copied the text of the four-part song which, approximately, reads: "But Amynt loves and says that nothing is so sweet. In my uncertainty I implore you; make your decision with common sense, my dear one. If love brings pleasure, it spells danger, Amynt prophesies to the Mother."

Thayer believes that this could be the text of the *Minnelied* (love song), namely of the Romance No. 4, and that the prose section could have been sung as a recitative. But Thayer is wrong; No. 4 is the "Romance," but the melody which he quotes is that of No. 2, the German song. Actually, the verses would be better suited to the Romance No. 4. If Thayer's assumption that the ballet music included vocal parts is correct, the relationship to equestrian ballets of the Baroque would be even clearer, because they also consisted of both vocal and instrumental music. Beethoven's *Ritterballet* includes a march, a German song, a hunting song, a romance, a war song, a drinking song, a German dance, and finally, a Coda. The main theme of the German song which Beethoven later used again for his Piano Sonata Op. 79, is repeated after the hunting song, the romance, the war song, and the drinking song. All the pieces are in the same key (D Major) like those of a suite; only the Romance, which has to be played pizzicato, is in B-minor. This melody reminds one of the song, *Im Mohrenland*, from Mozart's *Abduction from the Seraglio*; it is sung by the tenor, Pedrillo, and also called a Romance.

In his book, *Der Junge Beethoven* (Page 367) Schiedermair mentions the influence of Beethoven's Bohemian boyhood friend, Anton Reicha. The drinking song reminds us of the student song, "Meum est propositum in taverna mori," which Gottfried August Buerger paraphrased in the drinking song, "I want to die near the tap when the time comes." The "German Dance" has been explicitly named a waltz. Its melody reminds us of a melody from Saint-Saens *Carnival des Animaux*; it reappears in the Coda. This ballet represents the transition between the older suite and the dances which were new in classical times; their codas also resort to the melodic material of dances preceding them.

Far more important than Beethoven's *Ritterballet* is his music for the ballet, *Die Geschoepfe des Prometheus*, Op. 43. The choreographer Salvatore Vigano, a true successor of Noverre, had created a renaissance of the ballet in Vienna. The poet, Heinrich von Collin, described the situation of the Vienna ballet in those days (Collin's Works, Vol. VI, p. 305), and points out that the ballets, brought to their peak by Noverre and Angiolini, were revived during the regime of Emperor Leopold II (1790-92).

Antonio Muzzarelli (1744-1821) was a dangerous and effective rival of Salvatore Vigano. Muzzarelli had come to Vienna in 1791, as a Court choreographer and dancing master, and produced a number of successful ballets. When Vigano came to Vienna in 1793, the public, which suddenly discovered a consuming interest in the ballet, was split into two camps; like in Paris, during the controversy of the "buffonists," or the fight for supremacy between the respective followers of Gluck and Piccini, there developed a furious battle of opinions (Muzzarelli vs. Vigano). Collin believes that the most important state affairs would hardly have created such ardent factions as the rivalry between the two ballet masters.

Muzzarelli, who represented the older, more pedantic school, was defended in a short book by the dramatist and Field Marshal, Cornelius Ayrenhoff (1733-1819), *About the Theatrical Dances and the Ballet-Masters Noverre, Muzzarelli and Vigano,* which appeared in Vienna in 1792.

Ayrenhoff was in violent opposition to Joseph von Sonnenfels, the "Austrian Lessing," who strongly sided with Noverre. He was a reactionary in all things esthetic; to him, Shakespeare was a monster and Goethe's *Goetz von Berlichingen* a horror. His gods were Corneille and Racine. He took a similar position in his brochure about the dance; typical of his attitude about choreography was his insistence (page 42) that dances were only justified as an accompaniment to pleasant events "because, as natural expressions of cheerfulness, they turned into pantomimes."

As an example, he quoted Muzzarelli's ballet, *Otto II*, which had already been performed in Venice in 1785. "If the Empress and her daughter dance in the second act, they do so out of joy that their arrival in the Emperor's camp is welcome. This does not interrupt the tragic action which, prepared in the preceding act, now is halted until the Emperor and the prisoners return from the hunt." He cited Vigano's ballets as a contrast and used the *Semiramis* Ballet, "The Daughter of Air" as an example, even though it was written by Salvatore's father, Onorato Vigano (1739-1811) and performed in Vienna in 1793. In this ballet, the unfaithful Semiramis asks her deserted Memnon to a clandestine meeting; she sticks to her decision, to the torment of the cruel king. But all the while, so says Ayrenhoff, the pair dances phlegmatically, "the most tender pas de deux, as much apart from each other as the width of the stage permits." It is hard to judge in retrospect whether or not Ayrenhoff was biased when he made this statement. He forgot to mention that Vigano evidently wanted the dance to express the emotions of the pair.

The same piece, Ayrenhoff tells us, has a scene in which all the belles of the king's harem get dressed at the same time. "This would have been an excellent opportunity to show the audience a charming tableau of diversified, graceful poses, and groups of young women, partly seated, partly standing, but all somehow in motion. But Vigano? He lets them dance a pathetic chaconne, each holding a turban with a long veil in her hand, and, as they dance, they get dressed, following, as it were, the *Fliegelmann.*"

This comparison is the best example of the difference between Muzzarelli and Vigano. The former cared only for attractive movements, steps, postures; Vigano used the chorus as a means of expression. Collin believes that this was the reason for the victory of Vigano who led the dance from the exaggerated, empty artificialness of the older Italian ballet back to the simple, natural pattern. Instead of leaps, twisted limbs, and laborious positions without dramatic unity, there was action, emotional depth and unallayed beauty.

Collin was especially enthusiastic about Mme. Vigano (1756-1821). Her real name was Mayer, her pseudonym Maria Medina. Ayrenhoff elaborated on her work, he praised her facial expression but also mentioned her exaggerations which he called *Affereyen* (foppishness), "the way she showed her teeth, and abruptly turned her head and tossed it around in the manner of monkeys or, perhaps, mechanical dolls." These realistic movements, and the illusion of "nudity" which her attire created to perfection, may have had an even greater effect on a large part of the audience. She seems to have been especially realistic in the *Fille Malgardée*, which was given in 1794. Here her erotic pantomime must have created a sensation.

Salvatore Vigano was the head of a large family of dancers. His father's name was originally Onorato Braglia, but in 1754 he adopted his mother's maiden name of Vigano. Onorato's wife was the dancer, Maria Ester Boccherini, sister of the fa-

148

mous composer. Another son, Giulio, also became a well-known choreographer. Salvatore had his first instruction from his father, but considered thorough knowledge of composition essential for a dancing career, and began to study music with his uncle; incidentally, Onorato was also a composer. At 14, Salvatore arrived in Rome where his Intermezzo with music was performed—his only recorded composition. In Rome he also made his debut as a dancer—disguised as a girl because of his youthful appearance. In Rome women were not allowed to appear on the stage. A love affair in Florence brought him into conflict with a nobleman and caused him to go to Spain, where he met Maria Medina who thereafter shared most of his triumphs. He worked in London and Paris; then, as Revolution broke out, he went to Venice and from there to Vienna. Berlin and Dresden were only sidestops; Vienna always lured him back. Among Vigano's many ballets, the following are outstanding: *Raoul* (Venice 1791); *Richard the Lion-Hearted* (1795); *Giorgio* (1798); *Clothilde* (1799); *The Spaniards on Christina* (1802); *The Isthmic Games* (1803); *Benevento, Samete e Tamiri; Die Vestalin* (Milan 1818); also, the comic ballets: *The Sejour in Barcelona* (1794); *La Fille Malgardée* (1794); *The Magician Sisters* (1802); *The Discovered Violet* (1795); *The Vigilant Country Judge* (1800). Salvatore also set his father's ballets to music and danced them himself; among them is *Rinaldo ed Armida*. In 1793 he revised the ballet which Ayrenhoff mentioned: *The Daughter of Air*, or *The Elevation of Semiramis*. This ballet actually was Onorato's and Giulio had written the music; but Salvatore revised his father's sketch and added to his brother's music. As Vigano came to Vienna in 1793, his ballet, *Diana and Endymion*, or *The Triumph of Love*, was the greatest success of the ballet season; the choreography in the second part, the so-called, "rose-colored Pas de deux," was by Muzzarelli. Mme. Vigano was especially popular. Stendhal, quoting the famous *Eipeldauer-Briefe*, tells us that she was so greatly in vogue that pregnant Viennese ladies liked to wear little bellies a la Vigano. Her dances were always risque, especially in *La Fille Malgardée,* where the lover hides under the straw in the barn. A minuet a la Vigano, from G. B. Checchi's ballet, *Le Nozze Disturbate* (the Disturbed Nuptials), which was performed in Vienna in 1795, even pleased Beethoven who based Twelve Piano Variations on it (1795); the music was by Jakob Heibel, Mozart's brother-in-law.

In his essay, "Zur Wiener Ballettpantomime um den Prometheus" Robert Haas gave a survey of the ballet production in Vienna between 1791 and 1807; besides Muzzarelli and Vigano, it mentions the choreographers, Giuseppe Scalesi, Giuseppe Trafieri, and Francisco Clerico. Gaetano Gioia, the Frenchmen, Sebastian Gallet, Jean d'Auberval, Jean Coralli; and finally, Filipe Taglioni (1778-1871), the father of the great Marie Taglioni, also worked as choreographers in Vienna at the time.

Joseph Karl Rosenbaum—a well-to-do retired secretary of Prince Esterházy and married to the singer, Therese Gassmann —began a diary in 1797 and continued it to his death in 1829; he wrote about the première of The Prometheus, on March 28, 1801, that "The ballet did not please at all, the music little. At the end, the ballet was booed rather than applauded." Just the same, the ballet was not totally unsuccessful, for in 1801 it was repeated thirteen times, in 1802 nine times. Vigano's synopsis seems to have been lost; but the book, *Commentarii della Vita e delle Opere Coredramatiche di Salvatore di Vigano e della Coregrafia e de' corepei scritti de Carlo Ritorni,* (Milano 1838), contains a description of the ballet, parts of which were translated for the *Allgemeine Musik-Zeitung* of 1867 (p. 178), and also included in the Beethoven biography of Thayer-Riemann. The playbill of the premiere described the plot as follows: The basis of this allegorical ballet is the fable of Prometheus. The Greek philosophers, who knew about Prometheus, have described him as an exalted spirit who found his contemporaries in a state of ignorance, sought to improve their minds through the arts and scholarship, and taught them good deportment.

Based on this principle, this ballet shows how two statues

come to life and how the power of Harmony makes them receptive for all human passions.

Prometheus leads them to Parnassus to have them instructed by Apollo, the God of fine arts. Apollo orders Amphion, Arion and Orpheus to introduce them to music; he orders Melpomene and Thalia to acquaint them with drama and comedy; Terpsichore and Pan were to show them the bucolic dance which Pan invented, and Bacchus was to demonstrate his own creation, the heroic dance.

"The music is by Herr van Beethoven."

Ritorni's description reads as follows:

"The People of Prometheus, or, The Power of Music and Dance."

Pursued by the scorn of Heaven, which provides opportunity for a boisterous musical Prelude, Prometheus comes running through the forest, toward his two statues of clay. He quickly touches their breasts with the heavenly flame. Then, as he rests on a rock, tired and worried, the statues come to life. They begin to move and now really become what they always appeared to be: man and wife. . . . Prometheus starts up, looks at them with pleasure, invites them with fatherly affection to join him, but is unable to create in them common sense and responsibility; on the contrary, instead of turning to him, the two lazily drop to the ground, near a high tree. . . He tries again, with caresses and persuasion; but they, lacking the better part of human beings—common sense—don't understand his words and become grouchy; then they make awkward efforts to leave. Sadly, the Titan resorts to threats to hold them back, but to no avail. Now he becomes angry and tries to destroy his creation, but in his mind's ear he hears an exalted voice which stops him. His original mood returns, revealing that a new plan is taking shape within him. He grabs the two and drags them along.

The second act takes place on Parnassus. Apollo and the Muses appear; then come the Graces, Bacchus, and Pan with

151

his retinue; then Orpheus, Amphion and Arion, human beings yet to be born, introduced here as bold anachronisms. At the beginning of the scene, Apollo's Court shows a beautiful tableau of these poetic figures. . . Prometheus comes to introduce his children to the god, so that he might instruct them in the arts and sciences. Phoebus beckons to Euterpe; supported by Amphion, she starts to play, and to the sound of her melodies the two young creatures begin to show common sense and deliberation, to grasp the beauty of nature, to experience human emotions. Arion and Orpheus intensify the music with their citharas. . . . The creatures run hither and thither, and as they come before Prometheus, they recognize him as the object of their gratitude and love, prostrate themselves before him and embrace him passionately. Terpsichore arrives with the three Graces and Bacchus with his bacchants, and they perform a heroic dance. But the creatures cannot resist the lure of glory; they grasp weapons and want to participate at the dance! But Melpomene interferes and shows them a tragic scene: swinging her dagger, she demonstrates how human existence is terminated by death. She rushes to the astonished father, reproaches him that he has created the wretches only to make them experience such misery, and believes that death would not be too drastic a penalty. Prometheus' compassionate creatures try to protect him but she kills him with her dagger. Thalia interrupts this struggle with a comic scene, in which she covers the faces of the two lamenting creatures with her mask, while Pan and his fauns resuscitate the Titan; and so the play ends with a triumphant dance.

According to the playbill published by Thayer-Riemann, the premiere was a benefit for Maria Casentini (also called Cassentini), prima ballerina at the Vienna Court Opera at the turn of the century. She was Vigano's partner; his wife, Maria Medina, was no longer *persona grata* at Court, probably because of her over-zealousness to display her charms. Prometheus was danced by Cesari, Bacchus by Ferdinand Gioia, Pan by Aichinger, Terpsichore by Madame Brandi, Thalia by Cesari's wife, Melpomene by Madame Reuth. Apollo, Emphione, Arione and Orpheus were smaller parts.

Was Beethoven very proud of this composition? Aloys Fuchs, writing in the *Wiener Allgemeine Musikzeitung*, 1864, No. 39, tells the following anecdote: Haydn had heard the *Prometheus* music and praised it. Beethoven answered modestly: "Dear Papa, you are very kind. But the *Creatures of Prometheus* are by no means a *Creation*." Haydn seemed astonished and almost hurt. He replied: "This is true, it is not yet a creation—and I wonder whether it will ever become one"—whereupon the two parted, somewhat embarrassed.

We know that Haydn occasionally dubbed Beethoven a Great Mogul. In this connection, we may point out a small error of Thayer, which was taken over by Frimmel in his *Beethoven Handbuch*. Riemann also wrote in his essay, *Beethoven's Prometheus Music*, that the song, *Ich denke dein* (I think of thee) (Wo O-136), which was written in 1809, belonged to the sphere of the *Prometheus* music. This statement is based on a letter which Beethoven wrote to Breitkopf & Haertel, on June 26, 1809: ". . . You will soon receive the song, *Ich denke dein*, which had been intended for the hapless Prometheus. . . ." This, of course, does not refer to the *Prometheus* music, but to a magazine called "Prometheus," published by Leo von Seckendorff and J. L. Stoll in 1808. Quite apart from the fact that many years had elapsed since the premiere of the ballet, this song could not have had any possible connection with the *Prometheus* music.

Due to Ritorni's description, a fairly exact synchronization of music and action is possible. All told, the piece consists of 16 scenes and the overture. The first three scenes form the first act; the rest, the second. The overture, which starts with the dominate-chord of the seventh, like the Symphony No. 1, originally was entitled, *Tempesta*. However, it is not one of the customary descriptions of nature; actually, the overture seems to describe action and emotion simultaneously, that is, a powerful natural phenomenon, Man's development out of chaos and his liberation from the dark forces of the subconscious. But the overture also pictures the artist who strives for the most exalted attainments, following Goethe's titanism as expressed in his *Prometheus*-poem: "Did you every dry the tears of those pursued by fear? Has not all-powerful Time made a man of me?"

The first act is kind of a prologue. Prometheus wants to bring the two creatures to life and to have them share the blessings of culture. Since he can give them no more than mere existence, he takes them to Olympus where Apollo and the Muses should instruct them in the fine arts. The individual sections composed by Beethoven are mostly short movements which follow each other without interruption and fit the choreographic requirements.

Each of these movements was written as a separate, closed number, and little attempt was made at continuity in the work as a whole. The second act actually is a divertimento; its individual dances represent the various gods instructing the creatures in their respective arts.

Certain characteristics deserve to be mentioned: the $^6/_8$ meter represents the first faint ripples of emotion in the creatures. A harp—Beethoven used this instrument very rarely—accompanies the woodwind solo in No. 5; this number also contains a lovely cello cadenza and solo. An orchestral recitative is used when the creatures get dramatic instruction. Nos. 14 and 15 are solo dances in which the creatures exhibit their newly-acquired skills; the musical forms of these two movements are sets of variations. No. 14 contains a long solo for basset horn—a rarely-used instrument. The final number is a big dance ensemble of considerable musical interest, for Beethoven later used the main theme again for the finale of the *Eroica* Symphony.

But this theme does not appear only in the ballet and the *Eroica*; Beethoven also used it in a small contredance and as theme for the Piano Variations, Op. 35. Actually, before Op. 35 was published, Beethoven asked Breitkopf & Haertel that a reference to its use in the ballet be printed on the front cover. The use of the same theme in a ballet about Prometheus and in the heroic and noble *Eroica* leads us to wonder whether it had any extra-musical meaning for Beethoven. On the other hand, he undoubtedly was fascinated by the development potential of the theme and the accompanying bass. Obviously, he was not satisfied with its various treatments until he had completed the *Eroica,* and, significantly, never used it again.

The ballet is scored for classical orchestra, with paired woodwinds and the above-mentioned instruments added. The most striking feature is the frequent use of solo instruments and rare instruments, which may be attributed to the requirements of the drama and the nature of the music. But even though the music is excellent, the contemporary public never gets to see the ballet.

In his article, *Zur Geschichte der Beethovenschen Prometheus Ballett Musik (Zeitschrift fuer Musik-Wissenschaft,* Vol. 3), Robert Lach has mentioned that Vigano revised the ballet in 1813, and gave it the title, "Larger" Prometheus; in contradistinction to the original "Smaller" Prometheus. This ballet achieved considerable success. Ritorni gives a detailed synopsis:

This work had six acts, and the order of appearance of the characters differed from the original. The music was not exclusively Beethoven's; Joseph Weigl and others had contributed some of it. There also were quotations from the A-Major aria and part of the description of the chaos from Haydn's *The Creation,* and the earthquake from the *Seven Words of the Savior on the Cross.* This "Big Prometheus" was premiered at the Kärntherthor Theater, in Vienna, on November 18, 1843, in a new production by the choreographer, August Hus. Hus died in 1866. He had been ballet-master in Vienna from 1842 to 1844, and then went to La Scala, in Milan.

In Vienna, the music was put together by Matthias Strebinger (1807-1874), conductor of ballet music from 1822 to 1869. The synopsis, printed by Lach, is very elaborate and bursts with erudition and self-complacency. The title page says that the music was written by Beethoven and Mozart. In 1844, Hus performed *Prometheus* in Milan, and the printed scenario says that the music had been written by a number of composers; for instance, Act V by Anton Roht. It has been claimed that the "Larger" Prometheus has a number of advantages over Beethoven's original. It emphasized the theme of the antique myth; namely, the punishment and chaining of Prometheus and his torment, which Vigano had neglected. Instead of being punished immediately after he had stolen the heavenly flame, Prometheus is granted a short reprieve and indulges in merry company until the Cyclops lead him away.

The *Allgemeine Musikalische Zeitung*, of June 30, 1813, wrote about the new ballet as follows:

"Balletmaster Vigano, who has lived in Vienna for eight years and knows music well, deserves special mention: he uses German music almost exclusively (Haydn, Mozart, Beethoven, Weigl) and therefore must be regarded as an excellent sponsor of this kind of music in Italy. (We would only wish that he would leave the longer pieces as they are.) On May 22, after long preparations, he performed his *Prometheus* at the large theater here; it is in six acts, or, rather, large tableaux. The piece, written for Vienna and given there, was expanded, and received a far more splendid production. It is conceived on a grand scale (allegorical and symbolic) and its execution is truly exalted, especially in the first act which is the best."

"The underlying ideas of the six sections are as follows: 1. Man in his natural state, child-like but crude and wild. 2. Prometheus is enraptured with man and, wanting to raise him to spiritual perfection, steals the heavenly flame. 3. The effects of Man's exposure to the fire: the beginnings of society and of spiritual impulses; their development into passion, etc. 4. Their deterioration into envy, tyranny, etc.; Jupiter's wrath upon the dangerous benefactor of the mortals. 5. Happy consequences of human associations; higher education, the arts, matrimony. 6. Fulfillment of Jupiter's threats: Prometheus chained to the Caucasian Mountains, liberated by Hercules, restored in Jupiter's favor and included among the immortals. The whole has been turned into a clever pantomime; intricate machinery has helped to make the second act a superb production. The last four acts are less impressive, but they still have a few beautiful tableaux masterfully executed. It is a pity that Signor Landriani, one of our outstanding scene painters, had no part in this production. As a whole, the performance was extremely successful and a triumph for Signor Vigano. We know that Beethoven wrote the original music for the Vienna performance. Signor Vigano kept several of those numbers but replaced others with suitable and beautiful pieces by other composers—i.e. Ariel's aria in A Major and part of the chorus from *The Creation,* the earthquake from Haydn's *Seven Words,* a march by Weigel, and some numbers by himself. Several scenes are truly enchanting; to a degree hardly imaginable by anyone who has not seen the big ballets in Paris. The music enraptured the public, and the whole show may be called a triumph of German music in Italy. The production cost over 3,000 ducats. The Italian newspaper eulogized the performance and its originators; they also praised the music, but don't mention that it is German. For an Overture, Signor Vigano selected the one to Haydn's *Seasons.* Beethoven's piece had an indescribably strong effect."

"Since the preparation of the ballet took longer than expected, *Benevento,* also by Signor Vigano, was repeated; it had been written in Vienna and was performed here last year with great success. The music by Süssmayer, deserves much praise; it is among his best compositions—colorful, graceful and expressive. People here find it charming. Last year the piece had to be repeated for three full months, and everybody bought the score. An excellent Witches' Dance right in the beginning is sung by young and old, played on all kinds of instruments, resounds on all streets and squares. Pollini wrote and published pleasant variations on the melody."

* * *

A listing of Beethoven's works shows his great interest in dance music. His last quarters and piano sonatas give ample evidence that he often used dance rhythms in his compositions.

His Sonata Op. 79, starts with a *Presto alla tedesca—tedesca* probably meaning a quick Viennese waltz, not the more sedate laendler. Incidentally, the third movement of this sonata derives from the love song in the *Ritterballet* (See p. 145). A similar designation—*a la Danza Tedesca*—appears also in the Quartet Op. 130; in the presto movement of the Quartet Op. 131, a brisk *Zweischlagiger* whisks by, and the second part of this dance has to be played in the rhythm *di quattro battute*. According to Anton Schindler, the Viennese dance composers of Beethoven's time used to look down on his dance music, but it was not in Beethoven's nature to attribute much importance to this fact. According to Schindler, Beethoven's last effort in this direction dates from the year 1819, the year of the Missa Solemnis. At the inn *Zu den drei Raben* (in the suburb of Moedling where he then lived) he found a group of seven local musicians who played unadulterated country music. The friendship between them and Beethoven grew, and he wrote for them a number of dances—laendlers and others.

"I was present when Beethoven gave his newest opus to the leader of the small band at Moedling. This was in 1819. He mentioned cheerfully that he had organized the composition so that one or any other of the musicians could put down his instrument from time to time, take a rest or even a nap. After the leader had accepted the gift and left, Beethoven asked whether I had noticed how village musicians often dozed off as they played and then started up and came in with a few loud notes played at random, but mostly in the right key; so they alternated between napping and waking. In the *Pastoral* Symphony, he said, he had tried to imitate those poor fellows . . . dear reader, if you will look at the music on Pages 106, 107, 108 and 109 (of the Breitkopf and Haertel edition), you will find proof of this statement. You will find the stereotyped accompaniment by a phrase of the two violins (p. 105), the sleepy second bassoon with notes dropped abruptly, while bass, cello and viola have stopped playing. The viola doesn't wake up until p. 108; first it arouses its neighbor, the cello; then the second horn comes in, plays a few notes but passes immediately. Last to be fully aroused to renewed activity are the bass and the two bassoons. The clarinet, too, has a period of rest. The allegro in $^2/_4$ time (p. 110) borrows form and character essentially from old Austrian dance music; for in some of the old dances, the double rhythm suddenly changes to $^3/_4$ time. Having watched dancing folk in the woodland villages around Vienna (during the decade between 1820 and 1830), I have seen such dances performed. . . ."

Actually, the *Ländliche Tanz* (rustic dance) in the *Pastoral* Symphony seems indeed to be a highly stylized *Ländler*; the *Ländlers* played in Upper Austria and Styria show this transition from $^3/_4$ to $^2/_4$ time. What may be considered a confirmation of Schindler's report by an expert, was written in a book on *Ländlers* by Commenda, foremost authority on that type of dance: "Almost every fiddler or musician had his jealously guarded transcriptions of *Ländler* tunes; in many cases, handed down from generation to generation. Only an accomplished and learned musician could read these notes, and for the actual dancing, it was customary to play by heart. Most of the *Ländler* transcriptions, as well as those published from old records, are in $^3/_4$ time. The same musician may play the same melody in $^3/_4$ or $^2/_4$ time—following the pace set by the dancers."

The old "Grandfather Dance" begins with a deliberate, slow $^3/_4$ *Ländler*, and changes without transition into $^2/_4$ time. Such dances are still being used in the Austrian province of Salzburg.

Schindler further reports that Beethoven wrote a number of waltzes for the small band in Moedling, copying the parts himself. To trace these dances seemed a vain undertaking, and Schindler simply said that the score was lost. For a long time, this appeared to be correct, but in 1907, Hugo Riemann found the parts of these "Moedling dances" in the archives of the Thomasschule in Leipzig

All these Waltzes, Minuets, and *Ländlers* reflect the practice which Schindler pointed out; that the musicians were alternately sleeping and waking, as shown in the changing roles of the various instruments. Despite their relation to folk music, they are highly stylized, and Riemann mentions that the composer went far beyond the limitations of Austrian folk music and wrote genuine "Beethoven" dances.

Beethoven was fond of dancing, even though Ries tells us that he never managed to keep in step. This may have influenced the opinions of the Austrian dance composers who considered Beethoven's dance music unfit for dancing. But while music of those severe critics rest in music archives, unread, Beethoven's dance rhythms still delight the world. Nevertheless, many of Beethoven's dances were not re-edited or reprinted, and for the musicians of our time, they are practically nonexistent. The "Complete Works," Series II, contain 12 Minuets and 12 German dances (probably written in 1795); Series XXV (Supplement) contains six *Ländlerische Taenze* for 2 violins and bass, six German Dances for piano and violin, six German Dances for piano only, six *Ecossaisses* and some other dances. Series XVIII (Short Pieces for Pianoforte) contains six Minuets and 13 *Ländlerische Taenze* (Nos. 1-6 are identical with those of Series II, Nos. 7-12, and were preserved only for piano). However, we lack new practical editions.

Most of Beethoven's dances were written in a simple form resembling Mozart's. They are divided into eight parts, and based on few themes; the harmonic plan is also simple. Beethoven liked to borrow his own themes from earlier works; for example, in the "Moedling Dances" he used themes from his "Klavier-Bagatellen," and he quoted the accessory theme from the larghetto of his Symphony No. 2, in another dance in the same series. On the other hand, he transferred No. 7 of his Twelve Contredances to the *Eroica* and thus made it immortal. The most folk-like and popular of the dances are the Germans and the *Ländler*, which have a triadic melody and Alpine strains in the trio. Like Mozart, Beethoven closed his German Dances with a brilliantly developed long coda, returning to a theme of the last trio. The *Ländlerischen* are so realistic and primitive that they border on caricature, as in the piano version of Dance No. 3, when the bagpipe plays tonic and dominant simultaneously, which sounds like the tonic-dominant combination in the *Eroica*. In Dance No. 7, the accent on the second beat suggests the syncopated steps of peasants dancing the *Ländler*.

In his catalogue of Beethoven's compositions not included in the "Complete Works," Willy Hess mentioned a number of dances. But it seems more important to refer to Arnold Schering's controversial book about Beethoven's Symphony No. 7, which had been interpreted as a "dance symphony," Many saw in it the glorification of an autumn or harvest festival, as a sort of sequel to the *Pastoral* Symphony; others thought that it represented a wedding in the country. W. von Lenz agreed with the Russian critic, Seroff, who took it for a political military symphony; Robert Schumann was a follower of the "country wedding" theory which Richard Wagner ridiculed in his story, *Ein Gluecklicher Abend* (A happy evening) (1841). Wagner's own interpretation of the symphony as an "Apotheosis of the dance," which he expressed in his essay, "The Art Work of the future," is still valid.

Arnold Schering suggested a combination of the festival and dance theories and interpreted the symphony as a sort of esoteric program music in which Beethoven intended to illustrate individual scenes from Goethe's *Wilhelm Meister*. According to his reasoning, the first movement, with the intitial *poco sostenuto*, depicts the solemn arrival of the dressed-up children in the hall in which the actors have assembled; the *vivace* that follows is supposed to be Mignon's wild dance, accompanied by triangle and tambourine. Strangely enough, he takes the *allegretto* of the second movement for the Requiem for Mignon, because of the alternating singing of the chorus and the boys' ensemble; but this evokes the image of a danced exequy, in the sense of antique tragedy. Accordingly, the third movement, following a quotation of Philine in *Faust*, could be a

161

dance under the linden tree, and the fourth movement could present the merry, wild banquet in Wilhelm's room, where the actors have gathered around the bowl of punch.

In the Romantic school after Beethoven's time, the dance continued to play a very important part. Schubert's *Rosamunde Ballet*, whose action was written by Wilhelmine von Chezy, comes to mind. It was a failure, but its enchanting music is immortal and a separate book could be written about the many dances for piano and orchestra, and their treatment. This also pertains to Mendelssohn, who staged an Italian saltarello in the last movement of his symphony. In his *Carnival* Schumann resorted to the old suite of variations which he based on the letters "Asch"—the name of a small town in the Sudeten region where his first fiancee, Ernestine von Fricken, was born. We cannot elaborate on his many piano compositions, such as the *Faschingsschwang zu Wien* and the *Davidsbuendler-Taenze*. The Romantic movement was the starting point for the national schools of the 19th century, to which belonged Chopin, Smetana, Dvořák; the Russian, Spanish, Norwegian, Polish and South Slavic composers; and in those "Schools" dance reached its peak.

Let us close with a quotation from Goethe's *Tonlehre*: "Every organic movement manifests itself in systoles and diastoles—the expansion and contraction of heart and lungs." Our existence is based on them; and the great edifice of musical composition, which the occidental cultures built up in one and a half millenniums, started with simple movements, with the dance, which has an ever-lasting function in the history of music and which is responsible for the regeneration of an allegedly degenerated form of musical art.

INDEX

A

Abel, Carl Friedrich, composer, 26
Abert, H., 73
Abraham a Santa Clara, 110
Adam, A. Ch., 84
Affektenlehre, 14
Afflisio, Giuseppe, adventurer, 27, 68
Agata, Michele del, dancer, 71
Albéniz, I., 84
Alcina, ballet-opera by Handel, 17, 18, 19
Alfieri, Count, 39
Alladini, Eric, choreographer, 31, 74
Allard, Mme., 59
Almira, opera by Handel, 4, 5, 11, 12, 20
Amadigi, opera by Handel, 7
Amazaga, Marquis, 70
Anfossi, P., composer 134
Angiolini, Gasparo, 24-34, 35, 38, 53, 69
Arbeau, Th., 87
Arbuthnot, John, 23
Arend, Max, 35
Arie Styriache, 100, 134
Arie Viennesi, 67, 98
Ariodante, opera by Handel, 14, 15
Ariosto, L., Italian poet, 15
Artaria und Co., 130, 138, 139
Arteaga, Estéban, 24
Asow, Müller von, 79
Asplmayer, Franz, composer, 41, 68
Asselin, dancer, 73
Austrian Folkdances, 114
Ayrenhoff, C., 147

B

Bach, C. Ch. E., 36, 135
Bach, Johann Christian, 26
Bach, Joh. Seb., 36, 104, 135, 136
Badia, C. A., 66
Baif, J. A., 65
Balanchine, B., choreographer, 18
Ballet de Cour, 65, 66

Baroque Dance Festivals, 93, 96
Barthelemon, F. H., arranger, 31
Bártok, B., 140
Baton, Ch., 133
Battaglie (Battles), 129, 130
Batteux, Charles, philosopher, 30
Beard, John, singer, 19
Beccaria, Carlo, dancing-master, 66
Becking, G., musicologist, 127
Beethoven, Ludwig van, 32, 36, 55, 105, 112, 129, 143-162
Bernardi, dancer, 25
Bertali, Antonio, composer, 66, 78, 97, 144
Berton, Pierre-Montan, 40
Bertuch, F. J., 138
Binetti, Anna, dancer, 79
Blake, William T., 32
Blum, René, ballet-manager, 31
Blume, Friedrich, 84
Blümml, E. K., 102
Boccherini, Maria Ester, 148
Bois-Robert, French poet, 65
Bonno, G., composer, 69
Boucher, F., painter, 74
Bourrée, 5
Brahms, Johannes, 53, 123
Branle, dance, 87, 93, 106
Brenet, M., 140
Bretfeld von Kronenburg, J., 116, 133
Broessler, graphologist, 126
Brunelli, Antonio, composer, 33
Buerger, G. A., 146
Burlington Family, 23
Burnacini, Family of theatrical designers, 97
Burney, Charles, 15, 22, 36, 57
Burnonville, dancer, 42

C

Caccini, Giulio, 52
Cahusac, Lenis de, philosopher, 10, 20, 29
Caldara, A., 66, 97

163

Calzabigi, Raniero, 29, 33, 39, 51, 52, 53
Camargo, Maria Anna Cuppi, French dancer, 8, 9, 10
Campra, André, 5, 89, 90
Canal, Count E. J., 115
Canario, dance-form, 96
Cannabich, Chr., composer, 69
Caraccioli, Ambassador, 49
Carestini, G., singer, 11, 15, 17
Carey, Matthew, publisher, 32
Carpani, G., 137
Casacchi, dancer, 79
Casanova, Giacomo, 22, 26, 27, 34, 67, 68, 83, 117
Catherine de Medici, 65
Cavalieri, Emilio del, 66
Cesari, dancer, 150
Cesti, M. A., composer, 66, 78, 97, 144
Chaconne, dance-form, 4, 13, 37
Chambon, French publisher, 51
Chapman, G., 106
Charles VI., German emperor, 25, 100, 108
Checci, G. B., 150
Chedeville, E. Ph., virtuoso, 133
Cherubini, Luigi, 36
Chica, African dance, 85
Chrysander, Friedrich, 6, 11, 14, 15
Ciacchi, singer, 22
Cibber, Susanna Maria, 21
Clerico, F., 150
Coburg-Saalfeld, Fieldmarshal, 13
Collin, H. von, 146, 147, 148
Colloredo, Archbishop, 69, 123, 125
Contredance, 50, 85, 86 ff, 94, 128
Coralli, J., 150
Corf, Joseph, singer, 19
Corneille, P., 65, 147
Cornelys, Mme., cf. Pompeati, 26
Costa, José da, 4
Cotillion, 94 ff, 125
Cumberland, William, Duke, 22
Cuzzoni, Francesca, singer, 23
Czech Folkdances, 92, 119, 140

D

Dance Halls, 108-118, 139
Da Ponte, L., 118
Dauberval, J. (d'Auberval), dancer, 59, 73, 74, 150
De Falla, M., 84
Deller, Floria, ballet-composer, 33, 75
Delphin, Mlle., dancer, 53
Descamps, 42
Deutsch, O. E., 17
Diderot, Denis, philosopher, 29
Dies, A. C., 137

D'Indy, Vincent, 10
Ditters von Dittersdorf, Karl, 27, 46, 48, 101
Draghi, Antonio, composer, 45, 66, 78, 97
Dufort, I., dance-master, 88
Dumoulin, D., French dancer, 10
Duncan, Elizabeth, 48
Dupré, choreographer, 27, 71
Durazzo, Count Giacomo, 27
DuRoullet, Leblanc, 48, 57, 58, 60

E

Ebner, W., composer, 97
Edelbach, Herr von, 62
Einstein, Alfred, 59, 124
Elisabeth, Czarina, 26
Elizabeth I of England, 93
Elssler, Johann and Fanny, 140
Epinay, Louise, Mme., 72
Equestrian Ballet, 143, 145, 157
Erben, J., 75, 140
Eugen, Prince, 109

F

Falgera, Mme., ballerina, 82
Fandango, Spanish dance, 33, 34, 83, 84
Favart, Charles, playwright, 40
Favier, J., 68, 77
Fekete von Galantha, Count I., 111
Ferdinand, Archduke, 77
Ferdinand II., Emperor, 66
Fernando of Spain, Infant, 47
Feuillet, R. A., choreographer, 9
Feustking, Ch., Fr., Hamburg librettist, 4
Fischer von Erlach, 109
Florindo, opera by Handel, 5
Fokine, Michel, choreographer, 31
Forster, C. F., dancing-master, 89
Francis I., German emperor, 27
Fraz(s)i, Giulia, singer, 22
Freystaettler, F. J., 129
Friberth, Joseph, 46
Frimmel, Th., 153
Frischenschlager, Fr., 135

G

Gall, Josepha and Therese, 124
Gallet, S., choreographer, 150
Galuppi, Baldassare, composer, 26
Gamerra, G. da, 78
Gardel (Gardella), Family of dancers, 59, 70, 71

164

Garrick, D., English actor, 9, 20, 23, 37
Gassmann, F. L., composer, 69
Gavotte, dance-form, 18
Gay, John, 23
Gazzaniga, Giuseppe, composer, 31
Geoffroi-Bodin, Mme., dancer, 25
Geramb, V. von, 101
Gerber, Rudolf, musicologist, 49
German (Deutsche), dance, 86 ff, 134
Gigue, dance-form, 5, 13, 14
Gioia, G. and F., choreographers, 150, 151
Gluck, Ch. W., 3, 20-24, 25, 31-38, 54, 55, 59, 60, 68, 82
Goethe, Joh. Wolfgang, 29, 100, 102, 105, 147, 154, 161, 162
Goetz, J. M., publisher, 131
Goudar, Sara, 31
Graeffer, F., 112, 139
Graeter, F. D., 101
Granados, E., 84
Granier, Fr., 68
Granville, Mrs. Mary, 17
Grassalkowicz, A. Count, 137
Grassi, painter, 63
Grauer, composer, 20
Grenonville, French ambassador, 67
Grétry, A. E. M., 76, 103
Griesinger, G. A., 137, 138, 142
Grillparzer, F., 110
Grimm, Baron Melchior, 41, 49, 58, 70, 74
Grocheo, J. de, 106
Grün, Anastasius, poet, 22
Guacones-Dances, 4, 5
Gugitz, G., 112
Guillard, N. F., librettist, 60
Guimard Marie-Madeleine, 59, 73, 74
Gumpenhuber, Philipp, dancer, 26

H

Haas, Robert, musicologist, 32, 36, 133, 150
Habich, dancing master, 145
Hadow, W. H., 139
Haffner, S., 121
Halde, Père du, 37
Halfter, E., 84
Hamburg Opera, 3, 5
Handel, G. F., 3, 5, 6, 7, 12, 14, 16, 17, 21, 36
Hänsel, G., 88, 92
Harsdörfer, G. P., 144
Hasse, Faustina Bordoni and J. A., husband, 23, 35, 77
Haydn, J., 89, 105, 121, 133, 137-142
Heibel, J., 150

Heidegger, J. J., London impresario, 11
Heinel, Anna Friderike, 59
Heinisch, Theresa, singer, 46
Helfert, V., musicologist, 140
Hess, W., 161
Hildburghausen-Sachsen, Prince, 27, 45
Hiller, Joh. A., 41
Hilverding van Veven, Franz, choreographer, 23, 24-30, 45, 67
Hoboken, A. van, 138
Hoffer, J. J., 66, 97
Hofmann, C., 123
Holzbauer, Ignaz, composer, 25
Homberg, Historia Morali, 5
Hornpipe, 6
Howard, Andrée-Louise, choreographer, 18
Howard, Samuel, singer, 19, 20
Hummel, J. N., 131
Hummel, Margarete, 124
Huntington, Lord, 23
Hurdy-Gurdy, 133
Hus, A., choreographer, 155
Hyrtl, J., 140

I

Imer, cf. Pompeati, 22

J

Jacobi, J. G., 118
Jacquin, G. von, 115
Jahn, Otto, 73
Johann, Archduke, 114
Johnson, Samuel, 24
Jommelli, Niccolò, 35
Joseph II., Emperor, 47, 111, 129
Jozzi, Giuseppe, castrato, 22

K

Kanka, Joh., 116, 124, 134
Karl Eugen, Duke of Würtemberg, 71
Kauer, F., composer, 129
Kaunitz, W. A., Count, 135
Kelly, M., 103
Khevenhüller, Metsch, Prince, 29, 35, 48
Kirnberger, J. P., theorist, 36
Kozeluch, L. A., 131
Kröller, Heinrich, choreographer, 31
Kruthoffer, Franz, 39
Küchelbecker, J. B., 108
Kuhac, F. S., 139
Kurz-Bernardon, F. von, comedian, 103

L

La Borde (Laborde) , J.-B., 101
Lach, Robert, musicologist, 135, 155
Lacy, Fieldmarshall, 139
Lamberg, M., Count, 117
Ländler, 100, 104, 159-161
Lanner, J., 104, 113, 134, 138
Lany, Barthélemy, choreographer, 20
Lauchéry, E., 69
Lazzeri, Ghino, 29
Leger, dancer, 59
Le Grand, solo-dancer, 82
Leichtentritt, H., musicologist, 10, 11, 14
Lenau, N., poet, 134
Lenzi, dancer, 39, 41, 42
Leopold, Archduke, (Emperor Leopold II.) , 47, 146
Leopold I., Emperor, 67, 98, 143
Lepicq (Pick) , Charles, dancer, 42, 59, 68, 78
Lessing, G. E., 41
Leveridge, Richard, singer, 19, 20
Lobkowitz, Prinz Ferdinand Philipp, 21
Lodi, Pierre, dancer, 25, 26
Longman and Broderick, publisher, 31
Louis, XIV, King, 77, 88
Lully, J. B., 67, 77, 82, 89, 90

M

Malherbe, François, poet, 65
Malipiero, A. G., Senator of Venice, 71
Malter (Maltaire) , French dancer, 10
Maria-Amalia, Archduchess, 47
Maria-Josepha of Bavaria, 47
Maria-Magdalena, Archduchess, 96
Maria Ricciarda Beatrice, Princess, 77
Maria Theresia (Teresa) , Empress, 25, 38, 111, 135
Marie-Antoinette, 47, 57, 70
Marpurg, F. W., theoretician, 36
Martin y Soler, V., 105
Maschek, V., composer, 129
Matelot, dance-form, 5
Matteis, N., composer, 66, 97
Mattheson, Johann, 4, 14
Maximilian Franz, Elector, Archbishop, 144
Meissner, Alfred and Gottlieb, August, 116
Ménestrier, C. F., 97
Merk, dancing-master, 63
Metastasio, Pietro, 29, 35, 45, 78
Middlesex, Charles Sackville, Lord, 21
Minato, Nicola, Count, librettist, 45

Mingotti, Pietro, impresario, 39
Minuet, 12, 18, 86-91
Moldenhauer, Hans, 47
Monn, M., composer, 90, 91, 121
Monsigny, P. A., 76
Monteverdi, Claudio, 33, 66
Monticelli, Angelo Maria, castrato, 22
Morelli, dancer, 79
Moresca, Moorish dance, 16, 66
Moretto, dancer, 79
Morzin, Count, 137
Moser, Hans Joachim, musicologist, 32
Moylin, Francisque, 7
Mozart, Leopold, 68, 69, 72, 77, 91, 120, 125
Mozart, Nannerl (M. A.) , 120
Mozart, W. A., 31, 36, 48, 60 ff
Mueller, J. H., actor, 63
Muffat, G., 95
Müller, W., composer, 116
Murphy, Arthur, 37
Muzzarelli, A., choreographer, 146-148

N

Negri, Cesare, dancing-master, 28, 66
Negri, Maria Catharina, singer, 19
Nero, opera by Handel, 5
Nettl, Paul, 16, 26, 46, 75
Niemetschek, F. X., 119
Nissen, Nikolaus v., 62, 117
Nottebohm, Gustav, musicologist, 34, 126
Noverre, J. G., 9, 10, 20, 27, 33, 38-43, 53, 54, 68, 69, 71, 72, 73, 74, 147

O

Oettingen-Wallerstein, Prince, 138
Offenbach, Jacques, 31
Orel, A., musicologist, 133
Orestes, pasticcio, 14
Organ-concerto by Handel, 18

P

Pachta, Joh., Count, 116, 117, 128
Paisiello, G., 75
Pamer, M., composer, 113
Parini, G. A., 77
Parnasso in Festa, serenata by Handel, 11, 12, 13
Passacaglia, 5
Pastor Fido, opera by Handel, 11, 12
Paul, Sir J. D., 103
Pedrell, Felipe, 34
Pendarves, Mary (Delany) , 17

Peri, Jacopo, 52
Peslin, dancer, 59
Peter the Great of Russia, 97
Pfitzner, Heinrich, 60
Phillibois, Alexander, choreographer, 25, 26, 67
Piccini, N., 73, 74
Pichler, Caroline, 101
Pitrot, Antoine, dancer, 25, 26
Pleyel, I. J., 133
Pollini, F., composer, 157
Pompeati, Angelo, 26, 46
Pompeati, Teresa, singer, 22, 71
Pope, Alexander, 23
Porpora, Nicola, composer, 35
Pötting, Spanish Ambassador, 67
Preciso, Don, dancing-master, 85
Prévost, Françoise, French dancer, 7

Q

Quadrille, 95, 128
Quaglio, family of artists, 46, 50
Quantz, J. J., 89
Quinault, J. Ph., 54

R

Racine, J. B., 57, 77, 147
Rameau, J. Ph., 10, 11, 13, 18, 20, 57, 89
Ramm, Fr., oboist, 69
Reeve, W., musician, 31
Reicha, A., composer, 146
Reichard, H., 144
Reichardt, J. F., 38, 55
Reinhardt, Max, 82
Reuth, Mme., dancer, 153
Reutter, J. G., 137
Ricci, Antonio, dancer, 41
Rich, John, stage-director, 7, 9, 11, 12
Rigaudon, dance-form, 5
Rimsky-Korsakoff, N. A., 84
Rinaldi, Antonio, dancer, 26
Rinaldo, opera by Handel, 4, 6, 7
Rinck, E. G., biographer, 95
Ritorni, Carlo, 150, 151, 153
Robitschek, A., psychoanalyst, 94
Rodrigo, opera by Handel, 5, 11, 20
Rolland, Romain, 10
Rosenbaum, J. K., diarist, and Therese, (Gassmann), 150
Roser, F., and J. G., 131, 132
Roth, A., 156
Rousseau, J. J., 54, 57, 58

Rudolph, J. J., composer, 27, 33, 70, 75
Rudolph II., Emperor, 66

S

Sabbatini, Nicola, 66
Sachs, C., musicologist, 88, 104
Sachs, Hans, 110
St. Léon, A., choreographer, 83
Saint-Saëns, C., 146
Sallé, Marie, 6-14, 15, 17, 19, 20, 24
Salomone, Giuseppe, dancer-family, 25, 26, 78, 79
Salvi, A., librettist, 15
Saraband, dance-form, 4, 5, 12, 14, 18
Sarti, G., 128, 130
Scalesi, G., choreographer, 150
Schenk, E., musicologist, 68
Schering, A., musicologist, 161
Schiedermair, L., musicologist, 146
Schindler, A., 159
Schmeltzl, W., 110
Schmelzer, Joh. Heinr. and Andreas Anton, composers, 28, 66, 67, 97, 98, 100, 123, 133, 144
Schneider, M., musicologist, 83
Schottky, J. M., folklorist, 133
Schrattenbach, S. von, Archbishop, 123
Schubert, F., 105, 134, 162
Schumann, Robert and Clara, 55, 113, 161
Seckendorff, L. von, 153
Selden-Goth, Gisela, 141
Seroff, A. N., 161
Seyfried, I. von, 142
Shakespeare, William, 23, 24, 147
Simone, 43, 44
Simonet, dancer, 53
Sonnenfels, Joseph Freiherr von, 41, 147
Spanish dances, 82
Spontini, Gasparo, 45
Stampfer, dance, 91
Starzer, J., 26, 33, 68
Starzer, Katharina, singer, 46, 69, 75, 91, 121
Stendhal, 149
Stephanie, G., jun., librettist, 62
Stoll, J. L., 153
Stoppelaer, M., singer, 19, 20
Strada, Anna, singer, 15, 17, 19
Strasbourgeoise and Alsacienne, dances, 101, 102, 115
Strauss, Johann, 62, 104, 113, 129, 134, 138
Suessmayer, F. X.,
Swieten, Gottfried van, 36, 135
Swift, Jonathan, 23
Szabolcsi, B., musicologist, 140

T

Taglioni, Philipe and Marie, 150
Taubert, Gottfried, dancing-teacher, 4, 87
Terpsichore, ballet by Handel, 11, 12, 13
Tesi-Tramontini, Vittoria, 46
Thayer, A. W., 150, 155
Théodore, Mlle., dancer, 49, 50
Thompson, singer, 20
Timoschka, Russian dancer, 26
Trafieri, G., 150
Trancard, Antoine, 39, 43
Trénitz, dancing-master, 95
Tschudi, Th., Baron, 48, 49

V

Valse (Waltz), dance, 67, 86 ff, 103, 105, 118
Vanneschi, Francesco, librettist, 21
Veigl (Weigl), Eva Maria (La Violetta), dancer, 22, 24
Ventura, Santo and Domenico, choreographers, 28, 66, 67, 98
Verbunkos, 140
Vestris, dancer-family, 27, 68, 73
Vieth, Gerhard Ulrich, 34
Vigano, family of dancers, 20, 53, 146-157
Vismes, Academy-Director, 69
Voltaire, F. M. A., 9, 79

W

Wagenseil, G. Ch., composer, 91, 121
Wagner, Richard, 30, 55, 59, 161
Waldau, A., 119
Waldstätten, Baroness, 62
Waldstein, F. E., Count, 144, 145
Walsh, John, publisher, 24
Waltz, Gustavus, singer, 15, 19, 21
Watteau, A., painter, 74
Weaver, John, dance-master, 8, 9, 20
Weber, C. M. von, 104, 127
Weigl, J., composer, 155
Weller, German dance, 98, 100, 121
Wendling, J. B., flutist, 69
Wetzlar, Raimund, 62
Whaples, Miriam, musicologist, 5
Wilder, V., 74, 75, 76
Wilhelmine Friderike of Würtemberg, 138
Wolanek, A., musician, 116
Wolfram, R., folklorist, 114
Wotquenne, Alfred, 35
Wright, Mrs., singer, 19

Z

Zachow, F. W., 4
Ziani, Pietro Andrea and Marc Antonio, composers, 66, 97
Zingarese, dance, 138, 139
Zinzendorf, Karl, Count, 29, 37, 38, 111
Zoder, R., 101

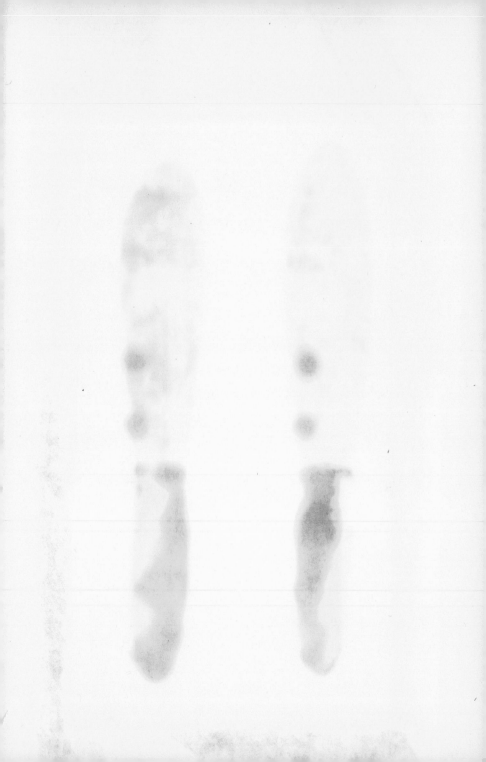

3-18-64

DATE DUE
